Marine Science for Kids

Exploring and Protecting Our Watery World

Includes **Cool Careers** and **21 Activities**

Josh and Bethanie Hestermann

Foreword by Stephanie Arne

Peachtree

CHICAGO REVIEW PRESS

© 2017 by Josh Hestermann and Bethanie Hestermann
All rights reserved
Foreword © 2017 by Stephanie Arne
First edition
Published by Chicago Review Press, Incorporated
814 North Franklin Street
Chicago, Illinois 60610
ISBN 978-1-61373-536-7

Library of Congress Cataloging-in-Publication Data
Names: Hestermann, Josh, 1983– author. | Hestermann,
    Bethanie, 1986– author.
Title: Marine science for kids : exploring and protecting our
    watery world includes cool careers and 21 activities / Josh
    and Bethanie Hestermann.
Description: First edition. | Chicago, Illinois : Chicago
    Review Press, Incorporated, [2017] | Includes
    bibliographical references and index.
Identifiers: LCCN 2016044402 (print) | LCCN 2017003058
    (ebook) | ISBN 9781613735367 (pbk. : alk. paper) | ISBN
    9781613735374 (pdf) | ISBN 9781613735381 (epub) | ISBN
    9781613735398 (kindle)
Subjects: LCSH: Marine sciences—Juvenile literature. |
    Marine sciences—Research—Juvenile literature.
Classification: LCC GC21.5 .H47 2017 (print) | LCC GC21.5
    (ebook) | DDC 551.46—dc23
LC record available at https://lccn.loc.gov/2016044402

Cover and interior design: Sarah Olson

Cover images: Coral: Jolanta Wojcicka/123rf.com; girl with
magnifying glass: courtesy of Jay Tayag; pelican: courtesy
of Bruce Fryxell; colorful fish: courtesy of Ülar Tikk; diver
Stephanie Arne, host of *Mutual of Omaha's Wild Kingdom*:
courtesy of Mutual of Omaha; crab and seal: courtesy of
Mark Gonka

Interior illustrations: Lindsey Cleworth Schauer

Printed in the United States of America
5 4 3 2 1

For Kim—
our mom and friend.

Contents

Foreword

Hi, all you animal lovers!

Ever since I was a kiddo, I felt a strong connection to animals and nature. My journey started with fun and engaging books about science and wildlife, just like this gem you're holding today. I remember seeing the pictures and reading the stories and becoming instantly obsessed with diving in the world's oceans.

Eventually my passion took me diving all over the world, to places like the Florida Keys, the Hawaiian Islands, Thailand, Africa, Australia's Great Barrier and Ningaloo Reefs, and all around the remote islands of Papua New Guinea, diving with cuttlefish, manta rays, and, my personal favorite, whale sharks. Each dive and travel experience opened a new door to the secrets of how humans and animals depend on each other for survival.

The more I studied the ocean, the more I saw how *everything is connected*. Whether you are a biologist, photographer, farmer, fisherman, or kid from South Dakota (like me!), your daily actions or creations can positively or negatively impact the health of all living things on the planet. Today, I get to share my knowledge and experiences with the world by hosting *Mutual of Omaha's Wild Kingdom*, an online video series about wildlife and conservation.

By reading *Marine Science for Kids*, you are starting your very own journey. I hope this book sparks a new passion in your heart and inspires you to use your specific talents and skills to help make our planet a healthier, happier place for generations to come.

Your friend,
Stephanie Arne
Host of *Mutual of Omaha's Wild Kingdom*
Founder of the Creative Animal Foundation

Stephanie Arne, host of *Mutual of Omaha's Wild Kingdom*.
Courtesy of Mutual of Omaha

Authors' Notes

On my 29th birthday, I was free-diving near a coral reef off the coast of Kauai, an island in the Pacific Ocean. Suddenly, I noticed a sea turtle gliding toward me. I tugged on my husband's leg to get his attention. Josh turned just in time to snap a couple of pictures as I swam alongside the graceful turtle. It was an unexpected moment that became one of my favorite birthday memories.

Some people say we know more about the moon than we know about our very own oceans. If you've ever wanted to be an explorer or an adventurer, then this is good news. There's so much left to explore right here on Earth! If you're a fan of cool, cute, or creepy creatures, then here's some more good news: some of the coolest, cutest, and creepiest creatures live just offshore in Earth's oceans and other watery places.

Sea turtles and other marine life deserve our appreciation. In some cases, they also need our help. I help by writing about science and conservation and educating the public about the issues facing our natural world. How about you? How will you use *your* talents to make the world a better place? As you read this book, we hope you will have some fun discovering just how much you have to offer. Happy exploring!

—Bethanie Hestermann, coauthor of
Zoology for Kids and *Marine Science for Kids*

~~~~~~

For as long as I can remember, I have tried to surround myself with water. Growing up in Arizona, I loved the way the desert smelled after it rained, I loved swimming in my backyard pool, and I loved visiting the beaches in California. I even ended up marrying a swimmer!

In college, I began researching sea lions on a tiny island off the coast of Mexico. During those trips, it was just me, my fellow researchers, a colony of California sea lions, hundreds of birds, and the big blue sea. It was these research trips that really made me fall in love with the ocean and everything it has to offer.

During my career as an animal caretaker, I have been lucky enough to work with marine mammals such as sea lions, harbor seals, gray seals, bottlenose dolphins, and sea otters, along with many animals that live on land. An important part of my job is to educate the public about issues marine mammals are facing in our oceans. Sometimes I get to participate in efforts to understand these issues. In one example, I traveled to Sarasota Bay, Florida, where I went out on a boat each day and helped perform health assessments on wild dolphins.

My wife, Bethanie, and I wrote *Marine Science for Kids* because we share a passion for Earth's water and all of the life that depends on it for survival—that includes you and me (and sea lions)! Getting to know playful sea lions was what hooked me into marine science. What is your hook? We hope this book inspires readers of all ages to find their "hooks" and then learn how to protect what they love.

—Josh Hestermann, coauthor of
Zoology for Kids and *Marine Science for Kids*

Bethanie and Josh pose with Paddles, a female Magellanic penguin. *Courtesy of Robin Riggs*

Time Line

AD 725 (circa) Saint Bede, an Anglo-Saxon historian, writes that the timing of the tides relies on the moon

1500 (circa) Leonardo da Vinci designs a diving apparatus for breathing underwater, but he never makes it

1735 John Harrison invents the chronometer, a portable timekeeping device that helps sailors determine their location at sea

1831–1836 HMS *Beagle* circles the globe with British naturalist Charles Darwin on board

1857 James Alden discovers Monterey Canyon in the Pacific Ocean

1869 Charles Wyville Thomson discovers deep-sea life in the Bay of Biscay at a depth of 14,610 feet (4,453 m)

1872–1876 HMS *Challenger* circles the globe conducting ground-breaking marine research

1906 Lewis Nixon invents a sonar-like underwater listening device to detect icebergs

1934 William Beebe and Otis Barton descend 3,000 feet (910 m) below the surface of the ocean in the bathysphere

1943 Jacques Cousteau and Émile Gagnan develop Aqua-Lung, a self-contained underwater breathing apparatus (scuba)

1953 Marie Tharp, a pioneer in mapping the seafloor, finds evidence of seafloor spreading by studying the Mid-Atlantic Ridge

1957 *The Silent World*, Jacques Cousteau's documentary about his oceanic research, wins an Academy Award

1960 Jacques Piccard and Don Walsh descend 35,814 feet (10,916 m) into the Mariana Trench aboard the *Trieste*

1962 Rachel Carson publishes *Silent Spring*, an influential book about environmental science

1970 The National Oceanic and Atmospheric Administration (NOAA) is founded to study Earth's oceans, atmosphere, and coastal areas

1972 A US Environmental Protection Agency ban makes it illegal to use the pesticide DDT

The Marine Mammal Protection Act becomes a law in the United States

1975 The Australian government creates a protected marine park around the Great Barrier Reef

1977 Scientists aboard the deep-sea submersible *Alvin* discover hydrothermal vent communities

1979   Sylvia Earle walks untethered on the seafloor at 1,250 feet (381 m) wearing a JIM diving suit

1985   Robert Ballard finds the *Titanic* shipwreck using a remotely controlled submersible called *Argo*

1989   Evelyn Fields, an African American woman, is appointed commanding officer of the *McArthur* and becomes the first woman to command a NOAA ship

1997   Charles Moore discovers part of what became known as the Great Pacific Garbage Patch

2008   NOAA commissions its ocean exploration vessel *Okeanos Explorer*

2009 (circa)   Rising sea levels force families to begin evacuating the Carteret Islands of Papua New Guinea

2010   The Deepwater Horizon oil rig explodes, spilling millions of gallons of oil into the Gulf of Mexico

2012   Canadian filmmaker James Cameron takes a solo journey to the deepest known point on Earth, the Challenger Deep

2012   An expedition captures first video of a live giant squid in its natural environment

2014   Researchers announce the scientific discovery of a deep-sea octopus that brooded its eggs for four and a half years

2015   The US government bans the sale of rinse-off products that contain plastic microbeads

2016   The US government expands the Papahānaumokuākea Marine National Monument to become the largest ecologically protected area to date

INTRODUCTION

What Is Marine Science?

Planet Earth is a vast, watery world, and the book in your hands is your ticket to discovering it. Now's your chance to slip below the surface of the ocean, where sunlit waters teem with life, and then dive to the bottom of the world, where real-life sea monsters roam in the darkness. What wonders await those who are brave enough to explore the sea?

Start your journey today by learning about **marine science**, the study of watery places, especially the ocean, and all the plants and animals that live there. As you read *Marine Science for Kids*, you'll get to know the marine environment by taking an imaginary stroll along the ocean floor, discovering how and why the ocean moves, and learning the answers to questions such as, why is the ocean blue? You'll get to know some of the coolest creatures on Earth by visiting coastal communities, the open sea, the deep sea, and rivers and lakes. Each turn of the page will unlock more secrets of the underwater world—and the world that surrounds it.

Understanding humans' connection with the planet is an important part of marine science. Later on in the book, you'll learn how humans are damaging Earth's watery places. *Marine Science for Kids* will challenge you to think about how humans can work together to protect the ocean and the animals that live there. Real-life marine scientists will share what inspires them to make a difference. If marine science is for you, you'll find some tips for turning your passion into a lifelong career.

In each chapter, hands-on activities—including science experiments, arts and crafts, edible projects, and games—make it even more fun to learn about marine science. Bake a cookie Earth, mold a miniature tide pool, race to clean up a pretend oil spill, conduct wildlife research—and this is just the beginning. Get ready to dive headfirst into the marvelous world of marine science. Who's ready to go exploring?

> See a bold word? Check the glossary for a definition.

A smiley elephant seal. *Courtesy of Bruce Fryxell*

Getting to Know the Marine Environment

Have you ever stood at the edge of the ocean, looking out across the endless blue, wondering what's out there? Pretend you're there right now. Your toes squish into the wet sand, and the sun is warm on your skin. A cool ocean breeze kisses your face. The air smells like salt and coconut-scented sunscreen. As the water pooled around your ankles gets pulled back to sea, your feet sink further into the sand. A wave comes crashing down and rushes past you with a *hissss*, spraying your shins with foamy seawater.

As you stand on the beach in your imagination, look out as far as you can. What do you see? Imagine that somewhere on the other side of the ocean, maybe thousands of miles away, there's another kid about your age looking out at the same endless blue. What lies between you and him may look like a bunch of nothing, but really, it's more than you can imagine.

For centuries, humans have gazed toward the horizon and wondered what mysteries the ocean holds. Some have sailed across it, returning home with tales of beautiful mermaids, salty pirates, epic

A view of the Pacific Ocean from San Pedro, California.
Courtesy of Mark Gonka

Aboard HMS *Challenger*

When HMS *Challenger* set sail from England in December 1872, the scientists on board had an enormous task ahead of them—to learn everything they could about the sea. *Challenger* sailed for nearly four years across all major oceans except the Arctic, perhaps because the wooden *Challenger* couldn't take on the icy waters.

Charles Wyville Thomson, the expedition's head scientist, and his team made observations and collected samples at 362 points along the journey. At each station, they measured the depth of the seafloor, took the water temperature, observed the speed and direction of ocean **currents**, and gathered samples of living things at different depths.

After the expedition ended in May 1876, scientists pored over the information and examined the samples brought back by the *Challenger* team. They compiled the results of the journey into a 50-volume report.

The 1872–1876 *Challenger* expedition was the first to accomplish ocean research on such a big scale. To this day, it is one of the most important events in the history of marine science. Even though *Challenger*'s crew did not have access to the same technology that scientists have access to today, much of the **data** they collected was accurate.

Earth's oceans and continents. *Courtesy of Jeffrey B. Vrieling*

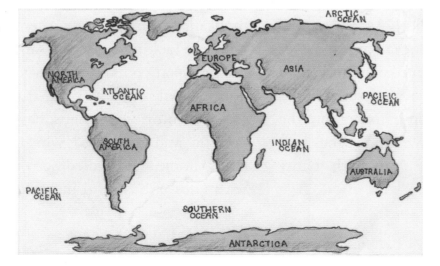

storms, giant swells, spooky shipwrecks, and slithery sea monsters. Others set out to sea and never came back at all. The ocean is a place of fantasy, adventure, and danger. It's a place full of wonder that raises more questions than it answers.

Humans are drawn to the sea because it makes us curious, but we also depend on it for food and other resources, as well as transportation. The ocean helps make life on Planet Earth possible. It absorbs heat from the sun and moves this heat around, keeping temperatures on land from becoming too extreme. The tiny marine plants that live in the ocean create oxygen that humans and other land animals breathe.

Even though humans can visit the underwater world, we haven't spent enough time there to know all of its secrets. Marine scientists, people who study marine science, help fill in the gaps by learning about the ocean, marine **ecosystems**, and marine life.

A Stroll on the Ocean Floor

If you could take a stroll along the ocean floor, would it be flat or hilly? Would there be tall mountains and steep cliffs like there are on land? By using **sonar** to map the seafloor, scientists know the answer to this last question is yes. Beneath the ocean's surface lie mountain ranges, volcanoes, submarine canyons, and **oceanic trenches** that dwarf the mountain ranges, volcanoes, and canyons on land.

Starting on the beach, if you walked straight out into the water, you'd be walking out on a

Bake a Cookie Earth

To understand why the ocean is so important, it helps to visualize how watery Earth really is. About 70 percent of the planet is covered by ocean, but to get a good sense of what this looks like, make some cookie calculations. Use a family sugar cookie recipe, or buy a package of sugar cookie mix.

ADULT SUPERVISION REQUIRED

YOU'LL NEED

- Sugar cookie dough
- Oven
- Parchment paper
- Flour
- Rolling pin
- Plastic bottle cap
- 2 cookie sheets
- Butter knife
- Blue frosting
- Green frosting
- Red frosting (optional)

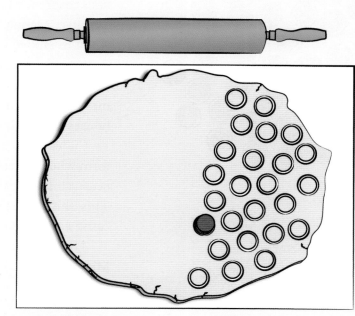

1. Prepare your cookie dough by following a recipe or the directions on a package of sugar cookie mix. Using a mix often requires adding butter, an egg, and a little bit of flour.

2. Preheat the oven to whatever temperature the directions on the package or the recipe indicates.

3. Spread parchment paper on a flat surface and sprinkle some flour on top. Use clean hands to place the dough on the parchment paper.

4. Roll out the dough with a rolling pin until it's about ½-inch (1¼-cm) thick.

5. Use a clean plastic bottle cap as a cookie cutter to punch 50 tiny cookie cutouts in the dough. It works best to press the bottle cap into the dough and then twist it a couple of times to make sure the cookie is separated from the rest of the dough.

6. Line two cookie sheets with parchment paper and place the tiny cookies on them, about an inch (2½ cm) apart. Two batches may be necessary.

7. Bake the cookies for about 8–10 minutes (time will vary depending on the recipe you're using), keeping an eye on them to make sure they don't get brown. Finished cookies should be firm when cooled but still light in color.

continued . . .

8. Place the cookies on a cooling rack or plate to cool.

9. Once the cookies have completely cooled, lay parchment paper down on a flat space for decorating and place the cookies on it.

10. Spread blue frosting on 70 percent of the cookies (35 cookies). The blue cookies represent ocean.

11. Spread green frosting on the remaining 30 percent (15 cookies). The green cookies represent land, including all of Earth's continents.

12. Next, place the cookies close together in a circle to represent Planet Earth. Place the green cookies so they look like Earth's continents and fill in the spaces with ocean cookies.

13. If you have red frosting handy, plot yourself on the "map" by making a tiny red X.

14. Take a step back and observe your cookie Earth. It's mostly blue, just like the real thing. Share what you've learned about the percentage of ocean versus land on our planet with a friend or family member. (Maybe share some cookies with a friend or family member too!)

Tip

Make this project simpler by baking 10 larger (2-inch, or 5-cm) cookies to represent Earth, or make it more difficult by baking 100 bottle-cap-sized cookies. In both cases, frost 70 percent of the cookies blue and 30 percent of the cookies green.

continental shelf, the edge of a continent that's covered by shallow sea. If you could keep walking, you'd eventually reach a steep slope called the continental slope, followed by a gentler slope called the continental rise.

Here, at the bottom of the world, you'd reach an abyssal plain, a large flat area that extends for miles. It would be dark and cold, and you'd be the only human in sight. If you walked far enough, you might suddenly find yourself at the base of a seamount, a huge underwater mountain. Many seamounts are former volcanoes.

Sometimes, active volcanoes grow so tall that they poke above the surface of the water and form islands. Mauna Loa, one of the large active volcanoes that make up the Hawaiian Islands, is a great example. Mauna Loa rises more than 30,000 feet (9,100 m) above the seafloor, though most of it is underwater. By comparison, the tallest mountain on land, Mount Everest, is about 29,000 feet (8,840 m) high, which is more than 1,000 two-story houses stacked on top of each other.

Underwater volcanoes and mountains often form where tectonic plates, large pieces of Earth's crust, shift, spread apart, or bump into each other. This shifting, spreading, and bumping can also cause earthquakes.

The longest mountain chain on Earth, the Mid-Atlantic Ridge, runs along a plate boundary in the Atlantic Ocean like a seam on a baseball. At this boundary, hot liquid rock wells up from the Earth's core, cools, and creates new seafloor as it slowly pushes the plates away from each other. Continents move along with tectonic plates, which

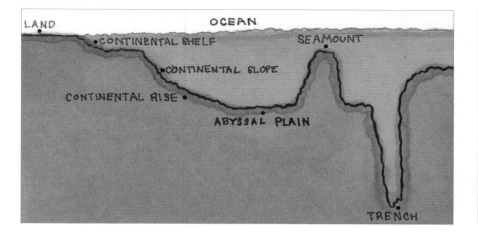

means the continent you're on right now is moving at about the same rate that your fingernails are growing.

Along with tall volcanoes and mountains, you'd also find some very deep places if you could take a stroll on the bottom of the ocean. When two tectonic plates collide, one gets pushed under the other, often forming a deep oceanic trench.

The Grand Canyon in northern Arizona is a mile (1.6 km) deep at its deepest point, but it is a mere dip in the landscape compared to the ocean's submarine canyons and trenches. The Mariana Trench in the Pacific Ocean reaches a depth of 6.8 miles (almost 11 km). That's more than six Grand Canyons deep!

While thousands of brave people have climbed Mount Everest, the highest point on Earth, only a few explorers have descended to the deepest known point on Earth, the Challenger Deep within the Mariana Trench. Such extreme deep-sea exploration requires a lot of high-tech equipment and a fair amount of risk.

All About Water

Water has the power to give life and to take it away. It can be cold, dark, and scary, but it can also be warm, bright, and clear. When you think of water, you might think of running through the sprinklers or diving off the high board into a deep pool, but water is not always a liquid. In fact, the same stuff you spray through a water gun also makes up puffy clouds in the sky and giant icebergs floating in the Southern Ocean. This is because water can be not only a liquid but also a gas and a solid.

Water is the only substance on Earth that exists naturally in all three states—liquid, gas, and solid. A single water **molecule** (H_2O) is made up of two hydrogen **atoms** bonded to the same oxygen atom, similar to the way magnets attract certain kinds of metal. A drop of liquid water is made up of billions of these water molecules that are grouped closely together, but not too closely. The molecules in a liquid can move past each other, which allows the liquid to flow.

(left) **Features of the seafloor.** *Courtesy of Jeffrey B. Vrieling*

(right) **Solid water makes up this iceberg, which is floating in the liquid water of Mikkelsen Harbor, Antarctica.** *Courtesy of Bruce Fryxell*

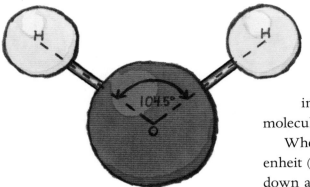

In a water molecule, two hydrogen atoms separated by a 104½-degree angle attach to an oxygen atom.

Courtesy of Jeffrey B. Vrieling

When liquid water warms up, the molecules start moving around so fast that they can no longer hold onto each other at all. When this happens, the liquid turns into a gas or vapor. In this form, the water molecules spread out and move around freely.

When liquid water cools below 32 degrees Fahrenheit (0 degrees Celsius), the molecules slow way down and hook together to form ice. In this solid form, the water molecules pack tightly together and can barely move.

One notable property of water is its **surface tension**. Far from being just a boring science term, surface tension makes it possible for some animals

to walk on water! The bonds that connect liquid water molecules together are stronger on the surface layer. These bonds create tension on the surface, as if a clear film were stretched across it.

When animals such as water striders and fishing spiders walk across a pond, their legs make tiny dents in the surface of the water, but the animals don't sink. The force of gravity pulling down on their bodies isn't enough to make them break through the invisible barrier created by surface tension.

Water molecules are good at dissolving other substances because one side of the molecule (the hydrogen side) has a slight positive electric charge and the other side (the oxygen side) has a slight

Water, Water, Everywhere

"Water, water, everywhere, / Nor any drop to drink." This is a line from a famous poem called "The Rime of the Ancient Mariner" by Samuel Taylor Coleridge. In the poem, sailors are stranded aboard their ship and become incredibly thirsty. They're surrounded by ocean water, but they can't drink a single drop of it. Why is it dangerous to drink seawater, even in desperate situations?

When humans drink seawater, a massive amount of salt ends up in our bloodstreams. Our bodies work hard to stay balanced, so when there is too much salt in our blood, water moves from the inside of our cells to the outside to try to correct the imbalance. Too much water leaving our cells causes them to shrink and become dehydrated. Our bodies' kidneys (organs that filter blood and help get rid of waste) try to flush the extra salt out of our systems by creating urine, which can further dehydrate the body.

If the sailors in "The Rime of the Ancient Mariner" drank seawater, they'd end up thirstier than they were in the first place. Their bodies would try to get back to normal, and by doing so, their cells would also be getting rid of the water they need to keep functioning. Eventually, if the sailors kept drinking seawater, they'd get headaches and become dizzy. In extreme cases, they could die.

Salt is not an enemy though. Humans' bodies need some salt to function. The amount of salt found in salty foods, such as crackers and soup, isn't nearly enough to be dangerous. However, if you've noticed that eating salty foods makes you feel thirsty, you're not alone. Your brain tells your body to drink more water when it notices that the bloodstream is a bit too salty.

Build a Water Molecule Model

Water molecules are called H$_2$O because they're made of two hydrogen atoms bonded to one oxygen atom. Build an oversized model of a water molecule to show off to your friends.

YOU'LL NEED

- Newspapers or a tablecloth safe for crafts
- 3 toothpicks
- Large (3-inch, or 8-cm) smooth foam ball (available at craft stores)
- 2 small (2-inch, or 5-cm) smooth foam balls (available at craft stores)
- Paint (two colors)
- Paintbrush and paint tray
- Glue
- Black permanent marker

1. Begin by covering your workspace with newspapers or a tablecloth that's safe for crafts. Poke the bottom of the each foam ball with a toothpick, leaving at least half of the toothpick sticking out of the foam.

2. Select a paint color for the oxygen atom. Pick up the larger foam ball by the toothpick and hold it like a Popsicle. Paint your oxygen atom and set it aside to dry.

3. Paint each of the smaller foam balls a second color to represent two hydrogen atoms. When you're done, set them aside to dry.
4. Once the paint on all three "atoms" is dry, remove the toothpicks.
5. Dab a bit of glue on the end of two toothpicks and insert them halfway into the two hydrogen atoms.

continued . . .

6. Dab some glue on the exposed end of each toothpick and carefully insert them into the oxygen atom at a wide 104½-degree angle. Refer to the water molecule illustration on page 6 for an example. It's OK to guess!

7. Use a black permanent marker to write an *O* on the larger foam ball to indicate oxygen. Write an *H* on each of the two smaller foam balls to indicate hydrogen.

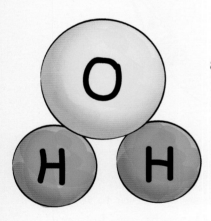

8. Show off your water molecule to a friend or family member and explain what happens as water molecules heat up and cool down.

Extra Credit

Research the answers to these questions: What is a covalent bond? What is a hydrogen bond?

---

negative charge. When you add a substance like salt to water, the water dissolves the salt by breaking apart the salt molecules.

If you've ever accidentally taken a gulp of seawater, you know that seawater tastes salty. In the ocean, the most common dissolved **minerals** are sodium and chloride. Together, sodium and chloride make salt. Marine scientists refer to the saltiness of the ocean as **salinity**. The saltier the water, the higher its salinity.

Water on the Move

In 2013, a kite surfer in Croatia came across a bottle on the beach, but this was no ordinary bottle. Inside it was a message that had been written in 1985, sealed in the bottle, and then tossed into the sea near Nova Scotia, Canada. The message read: "Mary, you really are a great person. I hope we can keep in correspondence. I said I would write. Your friend always, Jonathon, Nova Scotia, 1985."

For 28 years, Jonathon's message to Mary floated in the ocean, traveling from the eastern coast of Canada across the Atlantic Ocean, the Mediterranean Sea, and the Adriatic Sea, where it finally washed ashore in the European country of Croatia. Even though Mary never got his memo, Jonathon is one of countless people throughout history who hoped the ocean's movements would deliver his message in a bottle.

The ocean never stays still. Surface currents created by the wind move water on the surface of the ocean. When wind pushes surface water away from an area, colder, nutrient-rich water gets pulled

Why Is the Ocean Blue?

Have you ever wondered why the ocean is blue? The answer has to do with the way water absorbs and reflects light. Within each beam of white light exists all the colors of the rainbow. Each color humans see is actually a ray of light with a distinct **wavelength**. Of the colors humans can see, violet has the shortest wavelength and red has the longest. There are some wavelengths of light that humans can't see at all, such as ultraviolet and infrared.

A rainbow is proof that a beam of sunlight is actually made up of many colors. After a rainstorm, there's leftover moisture in the air in the form of millions of tiny water droplets. These droplets refract (bend) the light, separating it into its different colors and displaying stripes of red, orange, yellow, green, blue, indigo, and violet light across the sky.

When white light hits an object, the object absorbs some of the light rays and reflects others. Humans see the color or colors of the light waves that are reflected. When you look at a banana and describe it as yellow, it's because a banana reflects yellow light. If an object reflects *all* light wavelengths, it appears white. If an object *absorbs* all light wavelengths, it appears black.

What about the ocean? Large bodies of water absorb most of the longer (red) and shorter (violet) wavelengths but reflect the light waves we see as blue. The water molecules then scatter the blue light all around, which can make the water appear even bluer. When the ocean appears muddy, it may be because dirt or sand particles are reflecting other colors that combine to look brown. Along some coasts, the ocean may appear greenish-blue because tiny plantlike organisms called algae reflect green light.

up from the deep sea to replace it. This is called **upwelling**. Near coasts, the nutrient-rich water that upwelling brings to the surface helps support marine life on and near the continental shelf.

During El Niño events, winds that move surface water from east to west don't blow as much as usual. This reduces the amount of upwelling along the western coasts of North and South America and creates warmer-than-normal ocean temperatures in these areas. El Niño events affect wildlife because less upwelling means fewer nutrients for marine life.

Below the surface, where the wind can't reach, other forces such as temperature and salinity create movement in the ocean. Temperature and salinity affect seawater's **density**, the measure of how many atoms a substance has and how much space it takes up. Seawater rises or sinks depending on whether it's colder, warmer, saltier, or less salty than the water above and below it. Try the "Discover Water Density" activity on the next page to see how density relates to sinking and floating.

The movement created by differences in seawater's density helps form the Great Ocean Conveyor Belt. Like a river running beneath the sea, the Great Ocean Conveyor Belt brings cold water to warm places and warm water to cold places. The constant motion supports ocean life by moving nutrients from place to place.

Discover Water Density

Whether an object or a substance sinks or floats depends on its density. An object will float if it's less dense than the liquid it's placed in. It will sink if it's denser than the liquid it's placed in. Compare how different levels of salinity affect water density.

YOU'LL NEED

- 3 small clear drinking glasses
- Microwave
- 3 tablespoons of salt
- Spoon
- Blue food coloring
- Red food coloring
- Tall, skinny clear glass or small cylindrical beaker
- Syringe, eyedropper, turkey baster, or nasal aspirator

1. Fill three small drinking glasses halfway with tap water.

2. Put all three glasses in the microwave and heat them for about 1 minute (time will vary depending on your microwave). The water in each glass should be lukewarm.

3. Set the glasses in a row on a flat surface where you can work.

4. Add 2 tablespoons of salt to the first glass, 1 tablespoon of salt to the second glass, and no salt to the third.

5. Stir the salt in the first two glasses until the salt has dissolved completely.

6. Add four drops of blue food coloring to the first glass and stir.

7. Add four drops of red food coloring to the third glass and stir.

8. Carefully pour some water from the second glass into a new glass (a tall, skinny glass or a small cylindrical beaker works well). The skinny glass should be about a third full.

9. Fill a syringe, eyedropper, turkey baster, or nasal aspirator with the blue water from the first glass and use it to slowly add the blue water to the skinny glass.

10. Take a moment to observe. What happens to the blue water? Remember, the blue water has the most salt.

11. Add more blue water until a blue layer forms at the bottom of the skinny glass.

12. Next, slowly add red water to the skinny glass, using the syringe, eyedropper, baster, or nasal aspirator. What happens? Remember, the red water has no salt at all.

13. Add more red water until a red layer forms on the top of the clear water.

14. Now that you've seen density in action, try to answer this question: Which is denser, salt water or fresh nonsalty water?

Surfers are familiar with another type of movement in the ocean—waves. The wind creates most waves, which can be slow and rolling or choppy and rough. Other waves, such as tsunamis, form when a powerful force disturbs the water in the ocean. An underwater earthquake, a volcanic eruption, or a large landslide can trigger a tsunami, a series of large waves that can travel as fast as 500 miles (800 km) per hour. That's as fast as an airplane flies! When a tsunami reaches land, it often destroys everything in its path.

Ocean **tides**, the rise and fall of the sea, are another way the ocean moves. If you've ever built a sand castle high up on the beach only to have it destroyed by waves later on in the day, you've experienced ocean tides.

As the moon circles the Earth, its gravity pulls on the side of the Earth that's closest to it. By pulling the Earth and the ocean a little bit closer, the moon causes high tide on the side of the Earth that's closest to it and on the side of the Earth that's farthest away.

Most places on Earth experience two high tides and two low tides per day. For example, when high tide is happening at the top and bottom of the earth, low tide is happening on the left and right sides, and vice versa. During low tide, the ocean gets pulled back and the waves don't come up as far, revealing more of the beach.

Low tide is a great time to discover all the creatures that live in the stretch of beach between the tides. In fact, near-shore ecosystems are some of the easiest to study and explore because they are close to the coasts. Let's journey there now.

2

Coastal Communities

In the warm tropical waters surrounding a coral reef community, a bluestreak cleaner wrasse does a little jig. The vibrant fish has a long black stripe across its body and a bluish tail. As the wrasse zigzags around, swimming up, down, left, and right, it's sure to make a scene for all passersby.

As if called by the wrasse's dance, a moray eel, a fish-eating **predator** with a long snakelike body, emerges from its hideout. The eel slows as it approaches the bite-sized wrasse and opens wide its large, powerful jaws. Suddenly face-to-face with sharp teeth, the wrasse does something strange; it swims right into the eel's open mouth.

Hanging out in another fish's mouth—even one that's full of sharp teeth—is just another day in the life of a cleaner wrasse. Customers like the moray eel regularly show up at the wrasse's station looking for a cleaning, and the wrasse is happy to help.

The wrasse swims in and out of customers' mouths and **gills** and up and down their bodies eating mucus, bacteria, dead skin cells, and even parasites—unfriendly organisms living on a host animal's

A bluestreak cleaner wrasse cleans a moray eel's teeth.
Courtesy of Ülar Tikk

body. The cleaner wrasse vibrates as it works to remind customers that it's not food.

No funny business is allowed here at the cleaner wrasse's cleaning station. It's just an honest trade: one meal for one grooming session. The customers seem to get it. They even wait in line for the wrasse's services, as if they were waiting to buy groceries at a supermarket.

The cleaner wrasse and the moray eel are part of a dynamic coral reef ecosystem. Within reef communities, there are creatures that can regrow their arms or eject organs from their backsides, and there are even fish that can change from male to female or from female to male.

Coral reefs are some of the most popular places for marine life to live, but they are just one example of a coastal community. There are also underwater meadows and vast underwater forests filled with seaweeds that grow taller than trees! Within the ocean's diverse coastal communities, there's much to discover that's mysterious, wacky, and wonderful.

Reef Building

From space, astronauts looking back at Planet Earth—a glowing blue sphere suspended in blackness—can see what looks like splattered turquoise

Coral reefs may look like rocks, but they're actually made up of the stony outer skeletons of living animals called coral polyps.
Courtesy of Ülar Tikk

paint drops in the ocean near Australia. What they're actually seeing is the Great Barrier Reef, the largest reef community on the planet. The Great Barrier Reef is so large that it's like an underwater city. Unlike Chicago or Tokyo, however, this city is made up of the stony **exoskeletons** of tiny animals called coral polyps.

Each individual coral polyp has a soft body and a mouth surrounded by stinging tentacles that it uses to capture food. To protect their soft bodies, some coral species use minerals from the seawater to build up hard outer skeletons made of calcium carbonate, which is also known as limestone.

Polyps settle in by attaching themselves to something sturdy, like a rock on the seafloor or their neighbors' exoskeletons. There, they feed, build, and multiply, sometimes by creating clones or copies of themselves. As new polyps build up their skeletons on top of what other polyps have already built, they slowly construct a coral reef.

Coral reefs usually grow in warm, clear, shallow water where there's plenty of sunlight. Microscopic algae that live inside coral polyps depend on the sun to produce energy through **photosynthesis**. The algae share their nutrients with the coral, helping the polyps live and grow. The algae also give coral reefs their spectacular colors. From greens and purples to pinks and oranges, healthy coral reefs can be as colorful as a rainbow. They can also be oddly shaped. Some corals look like giant tabletops, while others look like spiky trees, fans, leather fingers, or even brains.

Thousands of creatures, from butterflyfish and pygmy seahorses to Christmas tree worms, depend

A pygmy seahorse blends in among the corals. *Courtesy of Ülar Tikk*

on coral reefs to find food and shelter. Along with all the other citizens of the reef, these animals must compete for the food and space they need while also defending themselves from predators. Each reef resident has special traits or **adaptations** that can help it do what it needs to do to survive.

Citizens of the Reef

Corals are part of a group of animals called invertebrates, which don't have backbones. An extraordinary number of other invertebrates live in the

Make an Edible Coral Reef

Coral reef ecosystems are full of color and life. Build a pretend coral reef made of puffed rice cereal (such as Kellogg's Rice Krispies) and melted marshmallows, add some "fish," and then gobble up your creation!

ADULT SUPERVISION REQUIRED

YOU'LL NEED

- 3 tablespoons of butter
- Large saucepan
- 1 package (10½ ounces) of marshmallows
- Stove
- Spatula
- 6 cups of puffed rice cereal
- 15-by-10-by-1-inch baking pan
- Parchment paper
- Cup of water
- Frosting and/or decorating gel
- Gummy fish candy
- Toothpicks

1. To make marshmallow treats,* melt 3 tablespoons of butter over low heat in a large saucepan.
2. Add 10 ounces of marshmallows to the saucepan. Stir the mixture with a spatula as the marshmallows melt.
3. Once the marshmallows have completely melted, remove the saucepan from the heat.
4. Slowly stir 6 cups of puffed rice cereal into the marshmallow mixture and continue stirring until the cereal is well coated.
5. Cover the bottom of a 15-by-10-by-1-inch baking pan with parchment paper to prevent the mixture from sticking.
6. Use the spatula to pour the marshmallow mixture into the baking pan.
7. Dip your clean fingers into a cup of water and use them to press the mixture down so it spreads out across the pan. (Water helps prevent the marshmallow from sticking to your fingers.)
8. Let the mixture rest for about 20 minutes, until it has cooled and hardened enough to hold a shape.
9. Spread parchment paper onto a flat surface, dip your clean fingers in the cup of water, and begin to mold handfuls of marshmallow mixture into different shapes—spheres, cylinders, or whatever you like. Stick the shapes together to create a basic structure for your reef.

10. Once you have the basic structure, use frosting and/or decorating gel to add some colors and patterns to your coral reef. Try mixing colors together or adding food coloring to white frosting to create new colors.

11. Add fish to your reef by sticking one end of a toothpick into the bottom of a gummy fish candy (such as Swedish Fish) and the other end of the toothpick into the reef.

13. Add a few more fish to finish up your coral reef ecosystem.

12. Admire, and then eat!

Marshmallow treat recipe adapted from www.ricekrispies.com.

sea. Sea anemones (uh-NEM-uh-nees) are marine invertebrates that often live on coral reefs. In the center of its spongy, tubelike body, each sea anemone has a mouth surrounded by fingerlike, stinging tentacles. Like coral polyps, anemones use these tentacles to stun and grab their **prey**.

Sea stars are other invertebrates that can be found on coral reefs. Sea stars often have five arms, but some species have many more. Sunflower stars, for instance, have up to 24. A sea star's important organs are in its arms, so if it loses one, it can regrow a new arm to replace the one it lost.

A hungry sea star wraps its body around prey, such as a clam, and uses its suction-cupped feet to pry open the prey's shell. Next, a sea star ejects its stomach into the shell and digests the soft body of its prey. Then the sea star pulls its stomach back into its body until it's time to find more prey and eat again.

Other reef-dwelling invertebrates called sea cucumbers may look like squishy cucumbers, but you won't find these odd creatures in a vegetable garden. Sea cucumbers living on coral reefs are often brightly colored, some with spots and some with spiky bumps. When threatened, a sea cucumber might eject an internal organ or two out of its backside to scare and distract a predator. This unusual

> Sea stars are not fish, they're echinoderms (ee-KY-no-derms), which is why scientists don't use the term *starfish.*

(top left) **A blue-barred parrotfish.** *Courtesy of Ülar Tikk*

(top right) **Can you spot the stonefish?** *Courtesy of Joel Warburton*

Flamboyant cuttlefish don't want to blend in; they want to stand out. *Courtesy of Ülar Tikk*

survival technique doesn't kill the sea cucumber because it can regenerate its lost organs later.

Alongside the invertebrates of the reef community live many species of fish. Fish are part of a group of animals called vertebrates—animals that have backbones, like humans. Most fish use gills to breathe oxygen dissolved in the water, and nearly all fish are **cold-blooded**, which means their body temperatures are the same temperature as their surrounding environments. There is at least one species that breaks this rule—the opah. These unique fish can generate small amounts of heat and distribute it throughout their bodies.

Reef fish are some of the most colorful in the world. Even their names are delightful—there are angelfish, clownfish, damselfish, parrotfish, and

Marine Reptiles

Most reptiles live on land, but some have adaptations for life in the sea. Sea snakes usually live in shallow, near-shore communities such as coral reefs. They have flat tails that help them swim and **venomous** bites that inject toxin into their victims. This venom helps sea snakes hunt small fish and other animals for food. While some sea snakes live their entire lives in the ocean, a group of sea snakes called sea kraits can also spend time on land. Banded sea kraits hunt in the water, but they rest, digest, and lay their eggs on land.

Banded sea kraits are venomous snakes that can live in the water and on land. *Courtesy of Ülar Tikk*

Seven species of turtles live in the ocean, including green turtles, leatherback sea turtles, loggerhead sea turtles, hawksbills, flatback sea turtles, olive ridleys, and Kemp's ridleys. Sea turtles have streamlined shells, long flippers, and webbed hind feet. Unlike many tortoises, sea turtles can't pull their limbs into their shells to hide. Sea turtles mostly live along tropical coasts in shallow waters, but some take long journeys across the ocean to build nests and lay eggs. Like sea kraits, sea turtles come to shore to lay their eggs.

The marine iguana of the Galápagos Islands is the only living lizard species that can survive in the sea. Though marine iguanas spend a lot of time hanging out on rocks and basking in the sun, they dive in the ocean to feed on algae and marine plants such as seaweed. Because they eat plants that grow in salt water, marine iguanas have a special trick to get rid of all the extra salt in their bodies—they sneeze! Marine iguanas have glands near their noses that expel (get rid of) salt. When the iguanas sneeze, salt goes flying.

Achoo! Marine iguanas sneeze to get rid of the extra salt in their bodies. *Courtesy of Ülar Tikk*

many, many more that live in coral reef ecosystems. A reef fish's colors and patterns may serve as **camouflage** by helping it blend in with the reef. One dangerously venomous fish, the reef stonefish, blends in so well that it can hide in plain sight. In fact, unless you look closely, it's hard to see a reef stonefish at all.

Colors and patterns may also help fish communicate. Unique patterns could help fish of the same species recognize each other. Bold colors and patterns can send a message to predators that a fish is dangerous. For example, a toxic species called the flamboyant cuttlefish flashes colors—often yellow, brown/black, white, and purple/red—to confuse predators and warn them to stay back.

Body shapes also vary on the reef. Some fish species, including trumpetfish and moray eels, are long and thin, allowing them to hide in crevices. A pufferfish can change its body shape thanks to its stretchy stomach, which allows it to inflate itself like a balloon. Spikelike projections called spines cover the bodies of some pufferfish, making them look less edible to predators.

Reef fish such as clownfish develop relationships with other organisms to protect themselves. Clownfish can live among the venomous tentacles of some sea anemones thanks to a layer of mucus on the fishes' skin that protects them from an anemone's sting. When threatened, clownfish often hide in anemones, and most predators don't follow.

Here's another fun fact about clownfish: they're all born male! Like several other species of reef fish, clownfish can change genders when needed to help their communities. When the female leader of a group of clownfish dies, a male from the group becomes female to take her place. Within species that have male-led groups, such as parrotfish, a female may change into a male to replace a leader that has died.

A coral reef is a gathering place for all kinds of interesting animals because it offers food and shelter. Like a city full of humans who look different from each other, perform different jobs, and have different life stories, a coral reef community is full of creatures that each have a part to play in keeping the ecosystem healthy.

(left) **Pufferfish have stretchy stomachs and can inflate their bodies like a balloon when threatened.** *Courtesy of Robin Riggs*

(right) **Clownfish can hide among the venomous tentacles of sea anemones.** *Courtesy of Ülar Tikk*

Pastures of the Sea

Some reef dwellers graze in nearby pastures called sea-grass meadows. Sea-grass meadows are important **habitats** because they provide food and shelter for a large number of organisms—from bacteria and algae to shrimps and crabs, salmon and herring, green turtles, and even "mermaids."

In 1493, Christopher Columbus, an Italian explorer, spotted three mermaid-like creatures while sailing near the Dominican Republic. He described the creatures as "not half as beautiful as they are painted." In reality, Columbus probably saw three manatees or their relatives, dugongs, and mistook them for the half-woman, half-fish creatures of lore.

Columbus isn't the only sailor in history to mistake these large, slow-moving **marine mammals** for mythical mermaids. With their humanlike eyes and tendency to bob up and down with their faces poking above the surface of the sea, manatees and dugongs are perhaps as close as explorers will come to finding mermaids in the ocean.

Manatees rely on sea grass for food, eating up to 150 pounds (68 kg) of it every day. Many fish also come to sea-grass meadows to lay their eggs among the grass blades. For this reason, sea-grass meadows are important as a nursery habitat.

Besides offering food and shelter and acting as a nursery for many marine species, sea-grass meadows are valuable to humans. Sea grasses produce oxygen through photosynthesis, they trap dirt and other sediment in their roots, which helps create cleaner coastal waters, and they help protect coastlines from storms.

Holding On: Life Between Tides

On rocky and sandy beaches between high tide and low tide lies the intertidal zone. In this habitat, hardy creatures have learned what it takes to hang on—sometimes literally—in an environment of extremes. The intertidal zone is underwater during high tide and exposed to the sun and air during low tide. Therefore, creatures that live in this environment must deal with changing temperatures, wind, and waves.

Hermit crabs, barnacles, mussels, limpets, and ribbon worms are a few of the organisms that can handle life in the intertidal zone. Barnacles keep from being swept away by the waves by creating a cement-like substance that anchors them to stable objects such as rocks and piers. Limpets move around but are able to hang on using a muscular foot and sticky mucus that acts like glue.

When the tide goes out on rocky beaches, water often collects between the rocks, creating mini-ecosystems called tide pools. In a tide pool community, organisms must be able to adjust to changing water temperatures, salinity, and oxygen levels. If you're lucky enough to come across a tide pool, be sure to stop and take a look! You might see sea anemones, sea stars, sea urchins, snails, or maybe even a small octopus.

Manatee or mermaid?
Courtesy of Joel Warburton

Mold a Miniature Tide Pool

Create four tide pool creatures using modeling clay and build your own miniature tide pool ecosystem.

YOU'LL NEED

- Newspapers or tablecloth safe for crafts
- Modeling clay (not the air-drying variety), at least five different colors
- Toothpick
- Trifle bowl, glass or clear plastic (available at craft stores), or a glass serving bowl
- 3–4 stones, suggested lengths of 3–5 inches (8–13 cm)

1. Cover your workspace with newspapers or a tablecloth that's safe for crafts.

2. Choose a color of modeling clay for a sea star. Sea stars come in every color of the rainbow, so pick your favorite.

3. Pinch off a piece of clay for the middle of the sea star and roll it into a ball that's about 2 inches (5 cm) in diameter. (Measurements throughout this activity are just suggestions. Feel free to make your tide pool creatures as big or small as needed to fit within your ecosystem.)

4. Pinch off five more sections of clay for the sea star's five arms and roll each into a fingerlike tube that's about 2 inches (5 cm) long.

5. Connect the five arms to the sea star's body and smooth over the edges. If you'd like, use a toothpick to add some texture to the sea star's body.

6. Choose a different color of clay to make a crab. Start with a piece of clay for the body of the crab and eight smaller pieces of clay for the legs.

7. Roll the crab's body into a flattened circle with a diameter of about 2 inches (5 cm) and then roll the eight smaller pieces of clay into skinny tubes for the legs. Attach four legs to one side of the crab and the other four to the opposite side.

8. Use two more pieces of the same clay to mold two large claws and attach them near the front of the crab's body.

9. Using white clay (if available), roll two small spheres and place them on the front of the crab's body for eyes. Roll two even smaller pieces of black clay (if available) into spheres and place one on each eyeball to give the crab pupils. (If you don't have white or black clay, you can substitute by using whatever dark color you have on hand and omitting the whites of the eyes.)

10. Next, use a new color of clay to mold a sea anemone. Form a chunk of clay into a cylinder—about 1 inch (2½ cm) in diameter—that's flat on the top and bottom. Using several small pieces of clay, mold the anemone's tentacles by rolling each piece into a skinny tube.

11. Use a toothpick to poke holes around the top of your anemone and carefully stick clay tentacles in each hole. If you'd like, poke one more hole in the middle of your anemone to represent its mouth.

12. Choose two colors of clay to create a limpet, a type of snail with a conical shell. Take a piece of clay from the first color and flatten it to make a pancake-like circle that's about 1 inch (2½ cm) long.

13. Pinch one side of the circle to make a small snail head. Use two tiny pieces of clay to add two small antennae to the top of the limpet's head.

14. Using the second color of clay you chose for the limpet, mold a cone-shaped shell with a flat bottom that's 1 inch (2½ cm) long. Place the shell on top of the limpet's pancake body. Add some texture to the limpet's shell with a toothpick.

15. Now that you have four tide pool creatures, decorate your tide pool ecosystem by adding some stones to your trifle dish.

16. Add your four clay invertebrates to the tide pool scene and fill the tide pool with water. See if you can remember or find a fun fact about each organism in your tide pool.

Extra Credit

Add at least two more organisms to your tide pool. For instance, add some green algae to the rocks and an octopus or a sea urchin to complete the scene.

Underwater Forests

In cool, nutrient-rich, and sunlit waters near coasts, tall seaweeds called kelp create vast underwater forests. Like a coral reef, a kelp forest is a near-shore ecosystem that supports an array of marine life. Unlike a coral reef, which grows very slowly, kelp forests can grow very tall, very quickly.

Along the Pacific coast of North and South America, and along the coasts of Australia and New Zealand, giant kelp can grow to be 120 feet (36½ m) tall, which is taller than most trees! The kelp anchor to the rocky seafloor and then grow up toward the surface. Gas-filled sacs called air bladders keep the kelp blades afloat.

Along the surface of the water, the kelp form a canopy. Within the canopies of some kelp forests, sea otters spend their days foraging for food, resting, and playing. Finding food is sea otters' top priority. Otters eat up to 25 percent of their body weight per day. If a 100-pound human were to do the same, she'd need to eat 100 quarter-pound hamburgers each day.

Since sea otters live in cold water, they have a thick fur coat to help them keep warm. In just one square inch of an otter's body, there can be up to a million hairs. Because their fur is so important to their survival, sea otters spend a lot of time grooming.

Whether they're grooming, eating, playing, or just floating on their backs, sea otters are fun to watch. Sometimes, otters wrap themselves in kelp to keep from floating away as they rest. A group of otters might also float side by side on their backs and hold hands, creating a "raft." This allows them to rest together.

Garibaldi fish, kelp bass, and types of rockfish are common in kelp forest communities. Some species' adaptations make them well suited to live among kelp. Kelp clingfish use their bellies and

> Otters are not just cute; they are an important part of the kelp forest ecosystem. You'll learn more about their role in chapter 6.

Mighty Mangroves

Mangrove forests are unique ecosystems that form in warm tropical and subtropical regions where the land meets the sea. Unlike many other plants, mangrove trees and shrubs can grow where it's muddy and salty. Mangroves benefit humans because their submerged roots stabilize coastlines, shield coasts from storms, and improve water quality. In the United States, mangrove forests exist along the Gulf Coast, especially in southern Florida.

Mangroves are home to some cool creatures, including lizards, snakes, and frogs, along with many species of insects and birds. The tangle of underwater mangrove roots is a great place for young fish to hide. Mangrove crabs, prawns, oysters, and periwinkles also live among the roots, where there is plenty of food and shelter.

Where India and Bangladesh meet at the Bay of Bengal lies the Sundarbans, the largest mangrove forest in the world. A unique community of organisms lives in this area, including fishing cats, Indian pythons, saltwater crocodiles, and Irrawaddy dolphins. At night, the lord of the Sundarbans, the **endangered** Bengal tiger, reigns supreme as the ecosystem's top predator.

fins as suction cups to stick to slippery kelp blades or rocks. Their grip is strong enough to hold on through currents and waves.

Among the seaweeds and sea grasses of southern Australia's coastal waters, leafy sea dragons' top adaptation is their camouflage. Cousins of seahorses, leafy sea dragons look like swimming decorations. The leafy appendages that stick out from their bodies make them easy to mistake for pieces of floating seaweed.

Even more creatures live on the kelp forest floor. This may include sea pens, nudibranchs (NOO-duh-branks), sea urchins, and crabs. The largest octopus in the world, the giant Pacific octopus, can also be found on rocky areas of the seafloor, including the kelp forests of the Northern Pacific Ocean.

Besides its permanent residents, a kelp forest, like other coastal communities, has frequent visitors—predators from the open sea that come to dine. The open sea is a vast ecosystem where some of the most exciting animals on Earth spend their lives traveling from place to place looking for food and mates.

(left) **Leafy sea dragons blend in among the seaweeds and sea grasses of southern Australia's coastal waters.** *Courtesy of Robin Riggs*

(right) **A giant Pacific octopus.** *Courtesy of Robin Riggs*

Promote a Coastal Community

Coastal communities are full of life because they are great places to live! Pretend you're in charge of recruiting new creatures to a coastal community. Your task is to make a brochure that promotes the benefits of living there. This activity requires access to the Internet or a library.

YOU'LL NEED

- 8½-by-11-inch sheet of cardstock (any color light enough to write on)
- Pen or pencil and paper or computer with word-processing software
- Printer (optional)
- Tape or glue (optional)
- Colored pencils and/or markers

1. Choose a coastal community highlighted in this chapter, such as a coral reef, a sea-grass meadow, a mangrove forest, or a kelp forest.
2. Reread the section that discusses your ecosystem and start to make a list of all the reasons an animal might want to live in the community you've chosen. Take note of some of the animals that already live there.

3. Complete your list by doing some research on the Internet or at a library. Try to answer the question, why do so many animals live in this coastal community? It could be that there's plenty of food, places to hide, or access to sunlight—or perhaps the water temperature is just right.

4. Feel free to be creative. For instance, you could say a benefit of living in a coral reef is "a colorful view out your window," even though fish don't care about having good views in real life.

5. Fold an 8½-by-11-inch piece of cardstock in half to create your brochure.

6. On the outer front page, write the name of your coastal community and, if you'd like, add a slogan. An example of a slogan for a mangrove forest community could be "Our Roots Run Deep!"

7. Add an image to the front of your brochure. You could draw a picture of your ecosystem or print a photo that you found on the Internet and glue or tape it on.

8. Inside your brochure, write a short paragraph about your community and why it's a great place to live.

9. In a new paragraph, describe some of the neighbors a new resident would have if it moved to your coastal community.

10. If you have room to spare, add drawings or photos of some of the neighbors and label them. Share your brochure with a friend, family member, or classmate.

Extra Credit

Test your knowledge of coastal communities by creating a brochure for each ecosystem mentioned in this chapter. What are the similarities and differences?

Life in the Open Sea

3

A pod of long-beaked common dolphins moves in perfect formation. The dolphins' sleek bodies slice through the water as their powerful tails pump up and down, propelling them forward. These normally playful dolphins are concentrated, coordinated, and on the hunt.

Ahead, a massive school of silvery sardines swims steadily forward. Despite being made up of thousands of individuals, the group appears to move as one. Out in the open ocean, predators might attack from any angle, but there's safety in numbers.

Click, click, click. The dolphins are coming. The clicking sounds are a product of the dolphins' **echolocation**. They're sending out sounds and then listening for the echoes as the sounds bounce off objects—in this case, fish. Echolocation helps the dolphins navigate underwater. It also helps them communicate with each other. *Click, click, click.* They're almost there.

From the left of the sardine school, the fish sense trouble—the dolphins have arrived. From the right and the back, more dolphins appear. The fish pack

Long-beaked common dolphins have sleek bodies that slice through the water.
Courtesy of Bruce Fryxell

themselves into a tight circle called a bait ball. They're trying to expose the fewest number of fish to danger. The dolphins swim circles around and below the bait ball; there's nowhere for the sardines to go but up, up, up.

The dolphins work together to force the fish toward the surface of the water. And then it's time to feed. One dolphin darts into the bait ball and grabs a mouthful of sardines. It swallows them whole. The next dolphin takes a turn, and then the next, and then the next.

From above, some seabirds want to get in on the action. The birds swoop and dive into the water to catch their share of the fish. When the dolphins have had their fill of sardines, they move on. What's left of the school swims down away from the surface, out of the diving seabirds' range, and the feeding frenzy is over . . . for now.

Sardines, dolphins, and seabirds are all connected as part of the **food chain**, the flow of energy within an ecosystem as organisms eat and are eaten by other organisms. For most animals living in the open sea, the food chain starts with ocean drifters called **plankton**, tiny unsung heroes of the sea.

Drifters, Swimmers, and Gliders

Meagan and Katie are at the beach. They've spent the day playing in the waves, and now they're building a sand castle. Meagan wants to add a moat, a water-filled ditch, to surround the castle. After the girls dig the ditch, Meagan fills a bucket with seawater and pours it in. Their moat is now filled with water . . . and what else? As you learned

(left) **Dolphins force fish toward the surface, and seabirds join the feeding frenzy.** *Courtesy of Bruce Fryxell*

(right) **A blue-footed booby bird.** *Courtesy of Bruce Fryxell*

Seabirds

Making a living at sea is tough business, especially if you are a bird. Of all the bird species on Earth, seabirds make up only a small percentage, but within this small percentage is some amazing variety. Seabirds include albatrosses, auklets, boobies, frigatebirds, gannets, penguins, puffins, shearwaters, and tropicbirds, among other groups.

Seabirds have adaptations that help them spend much of their lives at sea. When a seabird is soaring over the ocean, it's surrounded by salt water. So what does it drink? Seawater! Seabirds can safely drink seawater because glands near their eyes help remove extra salt from their bloodstreams.

Seabirds also have a variety of specially shaped bills that help them catch fish. Blue-footed boobies have sharp, pointed bills that the birds use to spear fish as they plunge into the ocean. Other seabirds have a hooked tip at the end of their bills, such as the wandering albatross, which has an impressive wingspan (the measurement from the tip of one wing to the other) of up to 11 feet (almost 3½ m).

Pelicans have large bills and a throat pouch that acts like a fishing net. When a pelican dives into the water, it scoops fish-filled seawater into its mouth, tips its head to drain the water, and then swallows the fish.

Most seabirds have webbed feet for swimming and waterproof feathers that help them float and stay dry. Some seabirds can fly for hours over many miles without needing to stop and rest. The Arctic tern has one of the longest **migrations** of any animal. Thanks to their special wing structure, Arctic terns can fly halfway across the world, traveling thousands of miles each year from the Arctic to the Antarctic and back.

Seabirds live longer than most other birds, and they tend to raise fewer young. Emperor penguins are doting parents that lay and care for just one egg at a time. After a female emperor penguin lays an egg, she travels to the sea to gather food. While she's gone, her male mate keeps the egg warm by balancing it on his feet, keeping it up off the Antarctic ice and next to his warm body until the chick is ready to hatch.

Since seabirds are an important part of the marine food chain, when there is a decline in seabird populations, it often means there is a problem with their food source—the ocean. Therefore, by studying seabirds, scientists can better understand the health of marine ecosystems as a whole.

Pelicans have large bills that help them catch fish.
Courtesy of Bruce Fryxell

Some fish, such as these humpback snappers, swim in large groups called schools. *Courtesy of Ülar Tikk*

these organisms are part of the most impressive migration on Earth.

At night, millions of organisms, including zooplankton, migrate to the surface layers of the sea to munch on phytoplankton before returning to deeper waters during the day. Some zooplankton move by pulsing their bodies; others use itty-bitty hairlike structures called cilia to push water past their bodies.

Why do marine scientists care about how and why zooplankton move? Since plankton form the base of marine food chains, they are massively important to life in the sea. The more scientists know, the better.

In addition to plankton, fish have also found homes in every corner of the ocean, from nearshore communities such as coral reefs and kelp forests to the deep sea. In between these extremes are tons of fish that live somewhere in the open sea, swimming from place to place, often in schools.

Herring, anchovies, and other schooling fish swim together to protect themselves from predators. When fish swim in a huge group, it is more difficult for predators to pick out where one animal stops and another one starts.

When rays—fish that have flat, pancake-like bodies, eyes on their topsides, and mouths and gills on their undersides—form groups, these groups are called fevers. Unlike most other types of fish, rays have lightweight, flexible skeletons made of cartilage, the same type of **tissue** that makes up human ears. Many rays are round, though some have long fins that look like wings. When rays swim, it's as if they're flying or gliding through the water.

in chapter 1, ocean water has dissolved minerals in it, such as sodium and chloride, but it's also full of living things.

The ocean is home to countless plankton that spend all or part of their lives drifting with the ocean's currents or, in some cases, swimming weakly. Plantlike organisms called phytoplankton include diatoms, a kind of algae. Another type of plankton, zooplankton, includes animals such as sea jellies, copepods, and krill.

Both types of plankton live nearly everywhere in the ocean, though they flourish near coasts. Phytoplankton drift near the surface of the water, where they can capture sunlight to create energy through photosynthesis. A day in the life of a zooplankton is a little bit more exciting. Every day,

Stingrays are a group of rays that have venomous barbs at the base of their tails. A ray's sting is a powerful defense against predators. The attack is painful and can be deadly. Electric rays have an even more shocking defense; they produce an electric charge that can deliver a strong electric shock to predators or prey.

Stingrays and electric rays are bottom dwellers that live in shallow habitats with sandy or muddy bottoms. Bottom-dwelling rays swim close to the ground or even bury themselves in the sand or mud. They have flat grinding plates in their mouths formed by fused teeth. These plates come in handy for crushing prey that have hard shells.

Other ray species don't stick to the seafloor; instead, they swim through the ocean column to strain plankton from the water. Manta rays tend to swim at or near the surface of the water, sweeping plankton into their mouths using fins that stick out from the front of their heads.

Manta rays and eagle rays are known for leaping out of the water, sometimes landing with a belly flop and a big smack. A PhD student named Joshua Stewart who studies rays at the Scripps Institution of Oceanography says when hundreds of these animals start leaping out of the water around you, it feels like you're sitting in a pot of popcorn as the kernels explode into the air.

The largest known ray, the giant devil ray, may grow to be 23 feet (7 m) wide, but these giants aren't the only large fish prowling the sea. Rays' cousins, sharks, also call the open ocean home.

Sharks: To Fear or to Revere?

In a famous scene from a scary movie called *Jaws* (1975), it's late at night and a teenage girl named Chrissie decides to go for a swim in the ocean. She runs down the beach and dives headfirst into the water as her friend trails behind. As Chrissie

(left) **Rays have flat, pancake-like bodies and flexible skeletons made of cartilage.** *Courtesy of Joel Warburton*

(right) **Some rays have long fins that look like wings, like this eagle ray.** *Courtesy of Joel Warburton*

swims out farther from shore, something grabs her legs and pulls her under the water.

The movie tells the imaginary story of a huge, vicious white shark (also called a great white) that terrorizes the beaches surrounding a small island community. Unfortunately, scary movies about sharks have given these creatures a bad rap.

While it is true that humans can be and have been hurt or killed by sharks in real life, it's important to remember that sharks—like lions and bears—are wild animals living in their natural habitat. It's also important to remember that not all sharks are big and not all sharks are dangerous. In fact, most sharks are small and harmless to humans.

Like rays, sharks have skeletons made out of cartilage, which keeps them light and buoyant. Unlike rays, sharks have streamlined, torpedo-shaped bodies with gill slits on either side of their heads.

Sharks have a highly developed sense of hearing and an incredible sense of smell. These animals also have senses that humans don't have. Like other fish, sharks have a **lateral line system** that helps them detect movement and pressure changes in the surrounding water. What look like small dots around a shark's snout are actually ampullae of Lorenzini, gel-filled pores that help the shark detect slight electrical fields given off by living things. A shark's extra senses help it hunt underwater with precision and accuracy.

Some sharks have sharp, jagged teeth that can easily tear into the flesh of their prey. Bottom-dwelling species such as zebra sharks have flat teeth perfect for crushing invertebrates such as snails and crabs. Sharks' teeth fall out easily, and an individual shark can lose and replace thousands of teeth in its lifetime. Since sharks have multiple rows of teeth in their jaws, when one tooth falls out, there's another one already there to replace it.

Tiny toothlike scales called dermal denticles cover a shark's body. On most sharks, dermal denticles lie flat and face the same direction, which helps them glide smoothly and silently through the water. Thanks to these dermal denticles, shark skin usually feels smooth one way (head to tail), and sandpapery the other way.

There are several hundred living species of sharks that vary greatly in size and shape. The smallest known shark species, the dwarf lantern shark, could fit in the palm of your hand, while the largest known shark species, the whale shark,

Sharks have streamlined, torpedo-shaped bodies. *Courtesy of Ülar Tikk*

would have a hard time fitting inside of a school bus. In the past, even bigger sharks may have prowled the sea, but they are now **extinct**.

Whale sharks, the largest living fish in the sea, eat plankton and therefore are not a threat to humans. In fact, most sharks present little threat to humans because they feed on small fish species and invertebrates such as crabs and shrimps. White sharks are among those shark species that feed on larger prey, including marine mammals such as seals, sea lions, and dolphins. Certain sharks might attack a human if they feel threatened, or they might take a "test bite" out of a human if they mistake that person for prey, such as an injured seal. However, shark attacks are very rare, especially when compared to other types of accidents involving humans.

Flippered Friends

Marine mammals are different from fish in many ways. Mammals have lungs and must hold their breath when they swim underwater, they have hair or fur during some stage of their lives, most give live birth and nurse their young, and they are **warm-blooded**, which means they can produce their own heat. Many marine mammals have a layer of fat called blubber that helps keep them warm.

Pinnipeds are a group of "fin-footed" marine mammals, including sea lions, seals, and walruses, that live partially on land and partially at sea. Sea lions are naturally curious, social pinnipeds that live in large groups called colonies. They're mostly found in the Pacific Ocean and on the rocky shores that border it.

Colonies are made up of females, their young, and a full-grown male that guards his territory fiercely. A sea lion colony is a noisy place because the animals bark loudly to communicate with each other.

Sea lions spend a lot of their time at sea catching fish, squids, and other marine creatures for food. A sea lion hunts underwater by taking a breath of air at the surface and then diving down, usually for just a few minutes at a time. If needed, they can hold their breath for about 10 minutes. During

> Some sharks lay eggs surrounded by a pillow-shaped egg case called a mermaid's purse. Other sharks don't lay their eggs; the eggs develop and hatch inside the mom shark's body.

Megalodon: A Predator from the Past

Perhaps the largest shark that ever lived was called *Carcharocles megalodon*, known simply as "megalodon." Scientists who have studied **fossils** of this extinct predator believe megalodon grew to be about 50 feet (15 m) long! Since sharks' skeletons are made out of cartilage, which breaks down more quickly than bone does, the only fossil record scientists have of these massive predators is their teeth, which are made of bone-like material that's strong enough to stand the test of time.

Besides estimating their size, scientists have also used megalodon tooth fossils to determine when the species lived. Current research suggests megalodon lived during a prehistoric era called the Miocene, which came after the time of the dinosaurs but before humans roamed the Earth. Scientists are still working on figuring out exactly when megalodon sharks went extinct.

The marine food chain during the era of megalodon would have looked different than it does today. Megalodon sharks likely hunted large marine mammals, especially whales. For this extinct ocean predator, it's a safe bet that anything and everything was on the menu.

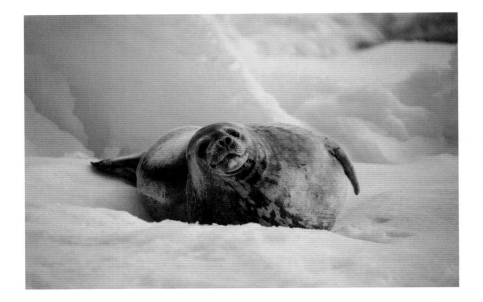

longer, deeper dives, a sea lion's heart rate slows down to help it use as little oxygen as possible.

Seals are pinnipeds that are sometimes confused with sea lions. Compared to sea lions, seals are rounder in the middle and have shorter front flippers, making them a bit awkward on land. Seals are swift swimmers, though, and they spend most of their time diving for food. An expert diver among seals, the Weddell seal, can dive up to 2,000 feet (610 m) and stay underwater for an hour. Most seal species live in the Arctic and the Antarctic, though there are exceptions such as monk seals and elephant seals.

Compared to the average seal, male elephant seals are massive and can grow to be about 20 feet (6 m) long. By comparison, a full-grown harbor seal is usually 6 feet (almost 2 m) long or less. Elephant seals get their name from the males' trunk-like snouts, which they inflate when they want to show other males that they're in charge.

Leopard seals can also grow quite large, but these Antarctic predators are especially unique because of what they eat and how they hunt. While other seals eat mostly fish, leopard seals are skilled hunters that go for larger prey such as penguins and other seals. Leopard seals are known to hide under the ice shelf and wait for penguins to jump into the water.

Walruses are Arctic-dwelling pinnipeds that have large, blubbery bodies, wrinkly skin, and whiskers that look like mustaches. Walruses use their sensitive whiskers to burrow around the seafloor looking for food such as clams and mussels.

Like sea lions, walruses live in groups and can be noisy. Both male and female walruses have two long teeth called tusks, which they sometimes use to haul their bulky bodies out of the water and onto the ice. A male walrus also uses its tusks to defend its territory against other males.

Call Me Sea Lion or Call Me Seal?

How can you tell if you're looking at a sea lion or a seal? Here are some tips. First, take a look at their ears. Sea lions have external ear flaps, kind of like humans, but seals do not. Next, compare their flippers. Sea lions have longer front flippers than seals. Underwater, sea lions rely more on their front flippers to propel themselves forward, while seals do the opposite by relying more on their hind flippers.

Sea lions can rotate their hind flippers beneath them, allowing them to walk and run on land. (Actually, a sea lion's run looks more like a gallop.) Seals can't rotate their hind flippers beneath them, so they must move around on land by scooting on their bellies.

You may also be able to tell a sea lion from a seal by taking a look at their fur, but not always. Most sea lion fur is a solid color. Many sea lions are chocolate brown, but some are blond. Seals usually have spots or other patterns in their fur. Ribbon seals, for example, have a unique fur pattern that looks like ribbons draped across their bodies.

Fur seals may be called "seals," but they are closely related to sea lions. Fur seals have all the characteristics of sea lions, but they also have a unique feature called underfur. Underfur is an extra coat of thick hair that grows beneath regular fur.

Fur seals often look fluffy because they have underfur. *Courtesy of Beverly Houwing*

Nature's Acrobats

Captain Abraham takes his boatful of paying customers out twice a day to go whale watching off the coast of California. Depending on the time of year, he might find gray whales, humpback whales, or even gigantic blue whales. Almost every day, he comes across a pod of dolphins.

Dolphins live in many different parts of the world's oceans. They have streamlined bodies, powerful tails called flukes, triangular fins called dorsal fins on the top of their backs, and long snouts called beaks. They breathe through a blowhole on the top on their heads. Dolphins are smart, playful, and often friendly to each other and to other species. They are also nature's acrobats.

When someone on Captain Abraham's crew spots a dolphin pod, the captain knows it's time to give his customers a good show. He asks the guests to take off their hats and hang on to the railing. The tourists squeal with delight as Captain Abraham speeds up the boat.

As the boat speeds up, the dolphins speed up too. They position themselves beneath the boat's bow and ride the waves coming off the sides of the boat as it plows through the water. Captain Abraham steers the boat in a wide circle and tells guests to keep an eye out for dolphins behind them.

At the back of the boat, passengers cheer. The dolphins are "surfing" in the boat's wake, the waves the boat creates behind it. One dolphin leaps straight up into the air, flicks its tail, and lands on its back with a big splash. Others jump in and out of the water together in a playful act called porpoising.

Dolphins, porpoises, and whales make up a group of marine mammals called cetaceans. Unlike pinnipeds, which live part of their lives on land, cetaceans live in the water full time. Some cetaceans swim very fast, some dive very deep, and some travel incredible distances underwater.

Dolphins seem to enjoy and rely on each other's company. They use echolocation to communicate with each other and to navigate underwater. To echolocate, a dolphin produces a series of clicks that passes through a special part of its body called a melon. The melon helps focus the clicks into a beam of sound.

Once a dolphin sends out this beam of sound, the clicks bounce off objects such as a boat or a group of sardines. When the sounds bounce back as echoes, fat-filled areas in a dolphin's lower jaw receive the echoes, which then travel from the lower jaw to a dolphin's middle ear and then to its inner ear.

Finally, a dolphin uses a dedicated part of its brain to interpret the sounds that bounce back. Using echolocation, a dolphin can determine the size and shape of objects and how far away they are. It may even be possible for dolphins to remember what the echoes from different species of fish sound like, allowing them to pick out their favorites from a group!

The largest member of the dolphin family is the orca, sometimes called a killer whale. Orcas have striking black-and-white coloration with a white patch behind each eye. They are one of many animals in the open ocean with bodies that are darker on one side and lighter on the other side. This adaptation is called **countershading**.

Pretend for a moment that you're floating near the surface of the water looking down into the darker, deeper waters below. An orca swims far below you, but you don't even see it because its back is black and it blends in with the background. Now, pretend you're a **scuba** diver swimming deep down in the ocean. If an orca swims above you, its white belly would blend in with the bright, sunlit water above you.

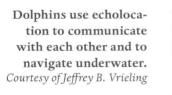

Dolphins use echolocation to communicate with each other and to navigate underwater.
Courtesy of Jeffrey B. Vrieling

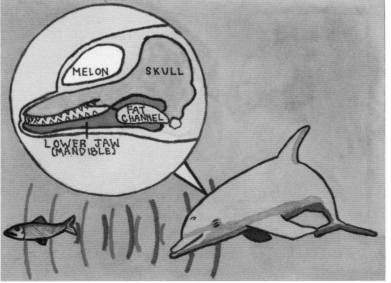

MELON SKULL

FAT CHANNEL

LOWER JAW (MANDIBLE)

Many other marine mammals, seabirds, and fish benefit from countershading, which makes it more difficult for them to be spotted from above and below. For an orca, a top predator in the ocean, its countershading can help it stalk prey more effectively. For creatures that are lower in the food chain, like a penguin, countershading can help them avoid predators.

Orcas have large teeth that come in handy when grabbing prey, including fish such as tuna and salmon and marine mammals such as seals, sea lions, and even other cetaceans. Like other dolphins, orcas use echolocation to hunt and to communicate with members of their pod.

Scientists recognize different types of orcas based on where the orcas live and what they eat. For example, in the Northern Pacific Ocean, there are "resident" pods that eat mostly fish, and there are "transient" pods that eat marine mammals. A third Northern Pacific group of orcas called offshores are the least well-known group because they live far away from coasts.

Closely related to dolphins is a second group of cetaceans called porpoises. Porpoises tend to be smaller than dolphins, with rounded heads and blunter snouts. A group of porpoises called finless porpoises lack a dorsal fin. One key difference between dolphins and porpoises is their teeth. While dolphins have cone-shaped teeth with pointed ends, porpoises have flatter teeth with rounded ends.

The future is unsure for a small porpoise called the vaquita. Vaquitas are native to the Gulf of California off the coast of Mexico, where their numbers have dwindled dangerously low. Because these endangered porpoises can become entangled in fishing nets, the Mexican government has placed restrictions on the types of fishing that can be done in the vaquita's habitat. As of this writing, international organizations and governments are working together to form a last-ditch effort to save the species from extinction.

(left) **Adélie penguins benefit from being dark on top and light on bottom.** *Courtesy of Beverly Houwing*

(right) **An orca.** *Courtesy of Bruce Fryxell*

Explore Marine Camouflage, Part I: Penguin Hide-and-Seek

For Adélie penguins living in the Southern Ocean, blending in is more than just a game of hide-and-seek. Their black backs and white bellies help them hide from predators such as leopard seals. Create a counter-shading wheel that demonstrates why a black back and a white belly help Adélie penguins survive.

YOU'LL NEED

- 6-inch (15-cm) salad plate
- Pencil
- 8½-by-11-inch sheet of white printer paper
- 8½-by-11-inch sheet of black cardstock
- 8½-by-11-inch sheet of plain white vellum (substitute parchment paper)
- Scissors
- Tape
- Pushpin
- Paper fastener/brad

1. Place a 6-inch (15-cm) salad plate facedown on a piece of white printer paper and trace the outline with a pencil.

2. Trace the plate's outline again on a piece of black cardstock and then again on a sheet of plain white vellum.

3. Cut out all three circles.

4. Fold the white circle in half both ways so the fold marks resemble a plus sign (+).

5. Cut the white circle into four equal pieces by cutting along the two fold lines.

6. Glue one of the white pieces to the upper-right section of the black circle so the curved edges line up.

7. Glue a second white piece to the lower-left section of the black circle so the curved edges line up.

8. The white part of the wheel represents the bright water a predator sees when it's below a penguin looking up toward the sun. The black part of the wheel represents the dark water a predator sees when it's above a penguin looking down away from the sun.

9. Draw the outline of a penguin (about 2 inches by 2 inches, or 5 cm by 5 cm) on a scrap of white printer paper and cut out the shape. The white cutout represents the belly or ventral side of a penguin.

10. Trace the penguin shape on a scrap of black cardstock and then cut out the second shape. The black cutout represents the back or dorsal side of a penguin.

11. Place the vellum circle on top of the black-and-white circle so they line up.

12. Set the black penguin cutout on the upper-right portion of the vellum circle so its head is facing the middle of the circle and its feet are facing the outside edge.

13. Set the white penguin cutout on the lower-left portion of the vellum circle so its head is facing the middle of the circle and its feet are facing the outside edge.

14. Tape the cutouts to the vellum.

15. Flip the vellum circle over so the penguins are on the bottom and line it up with the black-and-white circle.

16. Use a pushpin to poke a hole through the center of the vellum circle and the black-and-white circle.

17. Connect the two circles by pushing a brad through the hole and folding the prongs back.

18. Move the top (vellum) wheel around in a circle. What happens when the penguin's black back is against dark water? What happens when its black back is against light water?

Ocean Giants

The largest animal that has ever lived on Earth is swimming in the ocean right now. That means there is an animal alive today that scientists believe is bigger than extinct dinosaurs such as Tyrannosaurus Rex and even Argentinosaurus. What is this mysterious, gigantic creature that outweighs dinosaurs? A cetacean called the blue whale.

Blue whales are the ultimate ocean giants, weighing around 150 tons (300,000 pounds, or nearly 140,000 kg) and growing to be 100 feet (30 m) long. In 2014, scientists got an up-close look at a blue whale that had died after becoming trapped under unusually thick sea ice off the coast of Canada. A team from the Royal Ontario Museum recovered the 76½-foot (23.3-m) blue whale carcass, and scientists were able to measure and weigh the whale's heart, which was nearly the size of a golf cart. By comparison, a human heart is about the size of a closed fist.

Despite their huge size, blue whales eat tiny zooplankton, mostly krill. During certain times of the year, a blue whale can eat four tons (8,000 pounds, or 3,600 kg) of krill per day. Unlike dolphins and porpoises, blue whales don't have teeth. In the place of teeth, blue whales have **baleen**, stiff plates of coarse bristles attached to their upper jaws. Other baleen whales include fin whales, humpback whales, gray whales, and right whales.

A blue whale eats by searching out plankton-rich waters, opening its mouth, and taking a huge gulp. Folds of skin along its throat expand so the whale can hold even more water in its mouth. Next, a blue

Humpback whales are famous for singing songs and making big splashes. *Courtesy of Bruce Fryxell*

move closer together and up toward the surface. Then the whales lunge into the group of prey with mouths wide open.

Humpbacks migrate with the seasons, but the most well-known whale migration is that of the gray whale. One population of gray whales takes a long annual journey from summer feeding grounds in the Northern Pacific to winter **breeding** grounds much farther south. Sperm whales also take long trips, except they travel vertically, diving down to the depths to hunt for food.

Baleen whales are usually larger than toothed cetaceans such as dolphins and porpoises, belugas, and narwhals, but the sperm whale is an exception; these toothed whales can grow up to 60 feet (18 m) long. A sperm whale's unusually large, square head contains an organ that's filled with waxy fluid. In the past, humans hunted and killed sperm whales so they could use this fluid for candles, ointments, and other products.

Sperm whales are a link to the deep because they regularly dive between 1,000 and 3,000 feet (about 300–900 m) below the surface, possibly even deeper, using echolocation to hunt for medium and large-sized squids. Every once in a while, spectacular underwater battles take place between sperm whales and deep-sea dwelling giant squids.

Giant squids are just one of many remarkable creatures living in the deep that scientists know little about. Deep-sea exploration is an exciting area of marine science because new species are being discovered and described all the time. What other curiosities exist in the deepest parts of the ocean?

whale uses its gigantic tongue to squeeze the water through the sides of its closed mouth. Baleen acts like a pasta strainer, keeping the krill inside the whale's mouth as the seawater pours out.

Humpback whales are baleen whales that have long, narrow flippers. They're famous for their "songs"—their underwater moans and groans. They're also famous for their ability to jump out of the water and land belly-up with a giant splash. This behavior, called breaching, is exciting for whale watchers who are lucky enough to experience it.

Like blue whales, humpbacks eat by straining plankton and small fish from the water. They sometimes use a unique feeding method called bubble netting. To create a bubble net, one or more humpback whales swim in circles beneath a group of krill or fish and blow bubbles from their blowholes. The ring of bubbles forces the prey to

WHALE RESEARCHER

Asha de Vos, PhD

Founder
The Sri Lankan Blue Whale Project
Colombo, Sri Lanka

> "My most important responsibility is to leave the planet a better place than I found it."

As a child growing up in Sri Lanka, a small island nation off the southern tip of India, Asha de Vos was different. She wanted to be an adventurer, and she was fascinated by science. As she leafed through second-hand *National Geographic* magazines at a young age, it made her heart race just to think about the opportunities for adventure in the name of science. With the support of her parents, who simply said, "Do what you love, and you will do it well," Asha decided to focus on **marine biology**, the study of marine life, in college.

It was during a research trip that Asha first saw blue whales swimming in Sri Lankan waters. It was an experience that almost didn't happen. She had heard of a whale research vessel that would be stopping by her home country. Knowing how rare these opportunities were in her part of the world, Asha wrote to the owner of the boat, asking if she could get on board as an intern. He said no, but Asha didn't give up. She wrote again, explaining her desire to become a scientist who studies marine mammals. Again he said no. Determined as ever, Asha wrote to the boat owner every day for three months until he changed his mind and accepted her aboard the ship.

Several years later, Asha started the Sri Lankan Blue Whale Project. It is the first long-term research project on blue whales in the Northern Indian Ocean. Her goal is to scientifically understand the population and use science to help protect the whales in the long term.

Besides conducting scientific research, Asha spends a lot of time educating people about what she's learned. For example, she gave a speech at a TED conference, where some of the world's thought leaders come together to share their ideas with the public. During her talk, Asha made an argument for why everyone should care about whales and, specifically, whale poo, which helps cycle nutrients throughout the ocean. Her TED talk has been viewed more than a million times on the Internet.

Asha's message about whales' importance in the ocean may have spread far and wide, but her work isn't done. She works every day (with breaks to meditate, exercise, and spend time with her family) to protect blue whales and inspire the next generation of ocean heroes.

Asha de Vos, PhD.
Courtesy of Steve De Neef

Play the Lunch with Whales Game

Teeth versus baleen, do you know the difference? Explore lunchtime with whales as you and a partner take turns trying to catch some grub—cetacean style. This activity is best done outside or at a kitchen sink.

YOU'LL NEED

- Plastic water bottle
- Scissors
- Large serving bowl
- Water
- Measuring cup
- 1 cup of frozen peas (substitute frozen corn)
- Small cereal bowl
- Stopwatch/timer
- Fork

1. Carefully cut off the narrow end of a plastic water bottle. If there's a label around the middle of the bottle, remove it.

2. Cut five 2-inch-long (5-cm) slits along one side of the bottle, starting near the base. To make it easier, hold the bottle horizontally and give it a slight squeeze. When you do, the bottom of the bottle will bend into a V shape, giving you a nice surface to cut.

3. Fill a large serving bowl about halfway with water. If you're inside a house, place the bowl in the kitchen sink.

4. Measure 1 cup of frozen peas and pour them into the serving bowl. The peas represent krill, tiny zooplankton that live in the ocean.

5. Practice catching some "krill." Hold the bottle horizontally so the slits face down. Dip the bottle into the water and scoop up as many peas as you can.

6. Gently squeeze the bottle so the water pours out through the slits. Similar to baleen, the slits act like a strainer, keeping the peas inside the bottle.

7. When you're ready to play, place a small cereal bowl next to the larger serving bowl. If you're inside a house, place both bowls inside the kitchen sink.

8. Have a partner time you for 30 seconds as you catch as much krill as possible using the bottle strainer (baleen).

9. When your partner says go, scoop up some peas, strain *all* the water from the bottle strainer, and dump the peas into the small bowl. Repeat as many times as you can in 30 seconds.

10. After the 30 seconds is up, take a look at how much krill you caught before pouring the peas back into the serving bowl.

11. Next, try again, this time using a fork. The fork represents a whale or other cetacean with teeth.

12. When your partner says go, stab as many peas as possible and put them into the small bowl.

13. After 30 seconds, take a look at how much krill you caught this time around. Which adaptation, teeth or baleen, is most effective for catching krill?

14. Switch roles with your partner and play again.

Solve the Creature Mystery

Test your knowledge about the marine creatures mentioned in this chapter by solving a creature mystery. Play with a partner or two (see Rules for 2–3 Players) or with a group of up to 10 people.

ADULT MODERATOR RECOMMENDED

YOU'LL NEED

- *Marine Science for Kids*, chapter 3
- 13 small slips of paper
- Pen
- Bowl
- Tape

Objective

Gather clues by asking other players yes-or-no questions, and then guess which creature you pulled from the bowl.

Setup

Each player should take a turn reading about the animals listed on page 47 by finding them in chapter 3. Depending on the group, the adult moderator can decide whether players are allowed to reference the book after gameplay starts.

Write the names of the animals listed on page 47 on 13 slips of paper. Include the descriptors ("mammal/cetacean," "seabird," etc.) for beginners; leave them out for advanced groups.

Read each slip aloud before folding it and placing it in a bowl.

How to Play (4+ people)

Each player chooses a piece of paper from the bowl without peeking at what's written.

Tape each player's paper to his or her forehead so the players can't read their own animals but can read everyone else's.

Players begin by asking each other questions that can be answered with a yes or no. See the Tip box for examples.

When a player approaches another player, Player 1 should ask Player 2 a question, and then Player 2 should ask Player 1 a question before each moves to a new person. Players should avoid asking the same person two questions in a row.

Once a player is ready to guess her animal, she can ask another player, "Am I a(n) ____?" To which the other player can respond yes or no.

Players must ask at least three questions before making a guess.

After a player guesses her animal correctly, she remains in the game to help others by answering their questions.

The game ends when all players have guessed their animals correctly. Return the slips of paper to the bowl and play again.

Rules for 2-3 Players

After following the setup instructions, Player 1 chooses a slip of paper from the bowl. Without looking at the paper, Player 1 holds it to her forehead so the other player(s) can read what it says.

Player 1 asks the other player(s) yes-no questions until she has enough information to guess the creature. Player 2 goes next, then Player 3.

The players continue to take turns drawing slips of paper, asking each other questions, and solving the mystery until they've made it through all 13 creatures in the bowl.

Tip

When thinking about questions to ask, start with "Am I a fish?" "Am I a mammal?" or "Am I a seabird?" Then narrow down the options by thinking about animals' body colors, where they live, what adaptations they have, and what they eat. For instance, players can ask, "Can I go on land?" "Can I fly?" "Do I have tusks?" or "Do I eat plankton?"

blue whale (mammal/cetacean)

dolphin (mammal/cetacean)

elephant seal (mammal/pinniped)

megalodon (extinct fish)

orca (mammal/cetacean)

pelican (seabird)

penguin (seabird)

sardine (fish)

sea lion (mammal/pinniped)

stingray (fish)

vaquita (mammal/cetacean)

walrus (mammal/pinniped)

white shark (fish)

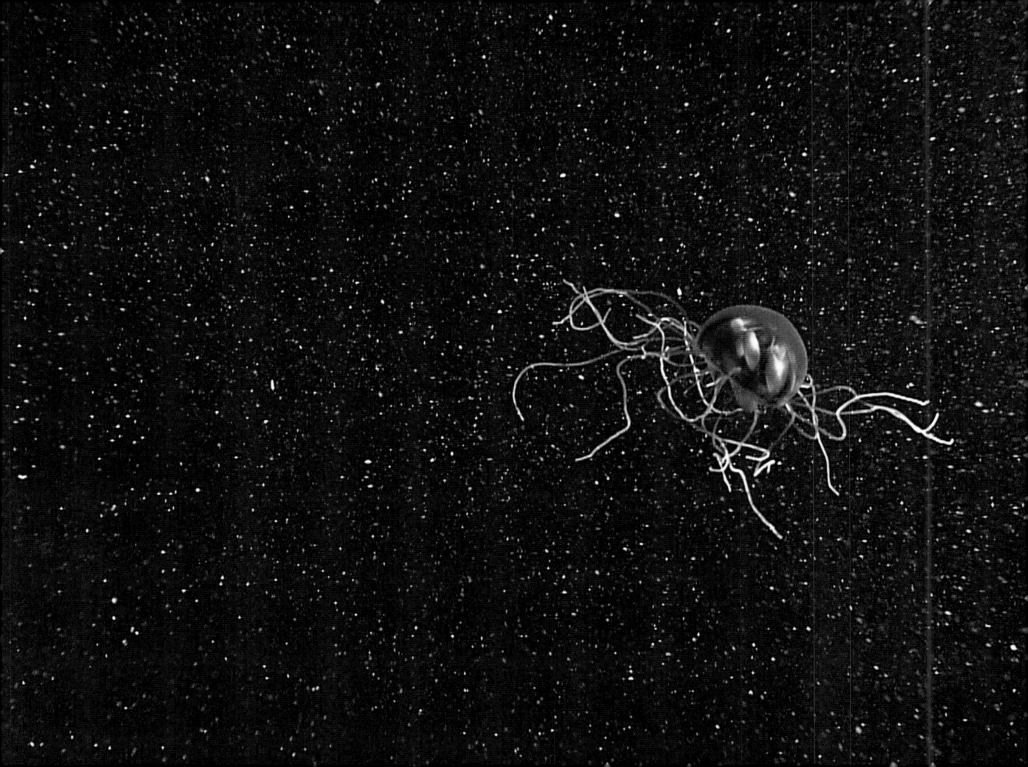

4

Diving Deeper

If the deep sea were a tourist attraction, the brochure might read something like this:

WANTED!

DEEP-SEA EXPLORERS! Are you looking for the adventure of a lifetime? Do you like really cold, dark places? How about shipwrecks and otherworldly sea creatures? If you like astonishing sights and don't mind cramped quarters, the deep sea is for you!

If this sounds dangerous and uncomfortable, it's because deep-sea exploration can be a little bit of both. But this hasn't stopped some marine scientists from making the ultimate dive to the bottom of the world. There, beneath miles of water, humans can't survive without special equipment—equipment such as a submersible, a device designed for underwater exploration.

At 1:15 PM on Thursday, September 22, 1932, aboard the *Freedom*, their mother ship floating off the

The deep sea is home to many incredible creatures.
NOAA Okeanos Explorer Program, Océano Profundo 2015: Exploring Puerto Rico's Seamounts, Trenches, and Troughs

coast of Bermuda, biologist William Beebe and engineer Otis Barton wiggled through a narrow 14-inch (36-cm) opening into a hollowed-out metal ball—a submersible called the bathysphere. Inside the bathysphere, the walls were about 4½ feet (1½ m) apart, barely big enough to hold Beebe and Barton's slender frames.

It wouldn't be a comfy journey, but it was a journey the two men were excited about. Beebe and Barton had coinvented the bathysphere and made several dives in it two years earlier, reaching 1,426 feet (435 m), a quarter mile below the surface. Now, they planned to dive even farther.

The two-ton bathysphere was round and made of heavy steel. Its walls were 1¼ inches (about 3 cm) thick. Two oxygen tanks supplied fresh air and two 8-inch (20-cm) windows would serve as peepholes to the alien world Beebe and Barton were about to witness.

Once the crew had secured the bathysphere's door with 10 big bolts, it was time. A machine aboard the *Freedom* lifted the bathysphere from the deck and lowered it into the water. As soon as the bathysphere splashed into the cold Atlantic Ocean, a surge of sea foam and hundreds of tiny air bubbles clouded Beebe's view from his window. Back on the *Freedom*, the crew began letting out a long steel cable that connected the bathysphere to the boat. As they let out the cable, Beebe and Barton began their journey into the depths.

By 2:37 PM, Beebe and Barton had reached 1,000 feet (305 m) down, where there is very little sunlight. Beebe later wrote in his book *Half Mile Down*

(1934) that it took some time at this depth for his eyes to adjust to the "blue-black gloom." At 1,426 feet (735 m), Beebe and Barton slipped past their previous dive record set in 1930.

As they continued to descend, the men used a spotlight to shoot a beam of light from the bathysphere into the blackness. Beebe spotted bronze sea eels and the pale green lights of lanternfish as they swam by his window. He saw the outlines of ghostly fish, some with eyes that shone with a dull glow. He even caught a glimpse of a fish that appeared to have long fangs.

Between 1,800 and 1,900 feet (about 550 m and 580 m), Beebe saw a school of large squids, the silhouettes of several big fish, and, mostly, an overwhelming sea of blackness. At 2,200 feet, Beebe described seeing hundreds of flickering lights, like sprinkles scattered across a sheet cake. The lights were dazzling; they made Beebe curious to know more.

After the bathysphere reached 2,200 feet, Beebe and Barton began their ascent back to the surface. Later, in 1934, they would go even farther, to 3,000 feet (914 m), just more than a half mile down. In the decades following Beebe and Barton's descents in the bathysphere, many other deep-sea explorers made daring, record-breaking dives in far more advanced underwater vehicles than the bathysphere. In 1960, Jacques Piccard and Don Walsh would descend 35,814 feet (10,916 m) into the Mariana Trench's Challenger Deep, the deepest known point on Earth. Piccard and Walsh made the journey inside a deep-diving research vessel called the *Trieste*.

Underwater Exploration

In the early to mid-1900s, French explorer Jacques Cousteau dreamt of swimming freely underwater. At the time, humans could explore the sea for only as long as they could hold their breath—unless they were in a submersible. Cousteau knew there was so much more to discover about the underwater world . . . if only he could access it.

In 1943, Cousteau and Émile Gagnan, a French engineer, invented Aqua-Lung, the first modern scuba device. Aqua-Lung made it possible for humans to swim deeper while breathing through a device that was connected to air storage bottles.

A few decades later, Sylvia Earle, an American marine scientist and explorer, took another big step for underwater exploration. In 1979, Earle walked untethered on the seafloor at 1,250 feet (381 m), a lower depth than any other human, in a device called a JIM suit that protected her from the extreme pressure. She explored for two and a half hours.

When scientists want to explore deeper—much deeper—they often use a remotely operated vehicle (**ROV**), an unmanned robot submarine tethered to a ship. The Monterey Bay Aquarium Research Institute (MBARI) is a world leader in deep-sea exploration. MBARI currently uses two ROVs, the *Ventana*, which can dive to 6,000 feet (over 1,800 m) below the surface, and the *Doc Ricketts*, which can dive to 13,100 feet—nearly 2½ miles (4 km)!

A fiber-optic cable connects an ROV to a ship, from which pilots can control the ROV's movements. Using an ROV's special equipment, including robot arms, sensors, and cameras, pilots can collect samples, gather information about the environment, and take photos and videos of the deep sea to share with the entire world. Using this technology, humans have captured rare images of deep-sea creatures like the vampire squid.

MBARI's robots have helped scientists discover and describe countless organisms in the deep. The ROVs have also made it possible to observe deep-sea creatures' behaviors in a way that was not possible before. In one example, researchers observed a deep-sea octopus brooding (covering and protecting) its eggs for four and a half years—longer than any known animal—as the eggs grew larger and the young octopuses developed inside.

MBARI researchers have used the *Ventana* ROV to explore the depths of Monterey Bay since 1989. *Kim Fulton-Bennett (c) 2014 MBARI*

Even after decades of discoveries, humans have explored only a small percentage of the ocean. Marine scientists studying the deep are like pioneers charting a new frontier. Each year, new marine species are discovered and described. Many of these new species live in the deep sea.

These explorations have given today's marine scientists a picture of what life is like in the deep—though it remains an incomplete picture. Once considered to be a biological desert where conditions were too harsh for life to survive, the deep sea has proved to be a fascinating ecosystem full of unimaginable creatures.

Conditions of the Deep

Light blue, dark blue, indigo, then blackness. This is how one deep-sea explorer, Graham Hawkes, describes the descent into the deep sea. Sunlight filters through the uppermost layers of the ocean, called the sunlit zone, but starting at about 650 feet (about 200 m), there's hardly any light at all. The section of the ocean from about 650 feet to 3,280 feet (1,000 m) is called the twilight zone. Below 3,280 feet is called the midnight zone. Since no sunlight reaches the midnight zone, it's like eternal night.

In general, the deeper you go in the ocean, the colder the water temperature will be. This is because there is less sunlight to provide warmth. In most parts of the deep sea, the temperature averages a few degrees above freezing all year long.

The deep is constantly under pressure. Pressure refers to a force pushing on all sides of an object or surface. On land, air presses on everything it touches—including you. You may not feel like you're under about 14.7 pounds (6.7 kg) per square inch of pressure right now, but that's because the fluids inside your body are pushing out with the same force as the air is pressing in on your body.

When the pressure around you changes, such as when you fly in an airplane, you can often feel the difference in your ears. This is because the pressure on the outside of your eardrum is changing while the pressure on the inside of your eardrum remains the same. When you "pop" your ears, the pressure equalizes and becomes the same.

Since water is denser than air, it applies more pressure on the objects submerged in it. The deeper you dive underwater, the more pressure there will be—and you don't have to dive far for the pressure to become noticeable. Swim to the bottom of a 15-foot swimming pool, for instance, and you'll probably feel a difference in your ears.

For every 33 feet (10 m) you dive underwater, the pressure pushing on your body increases by 14.7 pounds per square inch. Considering the ocean is thousands of feet deep in some places, the pressure adds up quickly. In the deepest parts of the ocean, the pressure is so intense it can crush a golf ball.

Scuba divers can dive deeper than regular swimmers because they bring a supply of pressurized oxygen with them, but humans can only go as far as their bodies can tolerate the pressure of an underwater environment. To dive in truly deep places, humans need the protection of a submersible.

Besides being dark, cold, and under pressure, there's not a whole lot of food in the deep sea. Luckily, there is **marine snow**, tiny bits of waste and debris that fall like snowflakes from the ocean's upper layers. Marine snow includes pieces of dead plants and animals, as well as feces (poop) from the creatures "upstairs." It might take weeks for a marine snowflake to drift all the way down to the bottom, if it's not eaten by one of many creatures living in the midwaters first.

Despite its name, the vampire squid is one creature that relies on marine snow (not blood) for food. These deep-dwelling cephalopods are reddish in color and have big pale-blue eyes. Cephalopods are a group of invertebrates that includes squids as well as cuttlefish, nautiluses, and octopuses.

Over centuries, sailors' reports of huge, deep-sea-dwelling cephalopods have given rise to the idea that a mythical sea monster called the kraken lives in the sea. Every once in a while, scientists get a tantalizing glimpse at a real-life "kraken." In the 1920s, colossal squid tentacles were found inside a whale's stomach. In 2007, off the coast of Antarctica, a fishing boat hauled a dead colossal squid on board. The squid's nearly 14-foot-long, 1,000-pound (4.3-m, 454-kg) preserved body is now on display at the Te Papa museum of New Zealand.

Then, in 2012, a group of scientists, including Japanese zoologist Tsunemi Kubodera and American biologist and deep-sea explorer Edith Widder, set out on an expedition to capture the first video of a giant squid in its natural habitat. The team used a camera system designed by Widder called the Medusa lander, along with a device called an electronic jellyfish, which acted as a lure by mimicking the natural light of deep-sea animals. The scientists suspended the Medusa lander and the

(left) **Marine snow includes pieces of dead things—and even poop—from creatures living above. Yummy?** *NOAA Okeanos Explorer Program, MCR Expedition 2011*

(right) **Vampire squids look a bit creepy, but at least they don't drink blood.** *(c) 2004 MBARI*

What's Special About a Cephalopod?

Cephalopods are cool. They're best known for having lots of arms, sometimes lined with powerful suction cups, but there's so much more to admire about this group of animals, which includes cuttlefish, octopuses, squids, and nautiluses.

Most cephalopods look rather squishy, but, surprisingly, they have a hard beak that can tear into prey. Many cephalopods are cunning hunters. Some cuttlefish, octopus, and squid species ambush their prey by waiting patiently until the prey is close enough to strike. Some even trick their prey into coming closer by dangling their arms as lures.

One of cephalopods' best tricks is changing their appearance, including the color and the texture of their skin. Some species use this trick to blend in with the background. Blending in has its advantages when stalking prey or hiding from predators. Like the flamboyant cuttlefish, other cephalopod species change the color and texture of their skin to do the opposite: to stand out. Dramatic colors and patterns warn predators to go away, or else.

Generally, cephalopods have three hearts and large brains relative to their size. Some octopus species are smart enough to solve basic puzzles, such as how to unscrew a jar from the inside. Cephalopods may use their arms to swim or even "walk" along the seafloor, but if they need to get somewhere in a hurry, they use jet propulsion. By filling its mantle, a cavity near its head, with water and then forcing the water out through a tube, the animal can make a quick escape.

When threatened, some cephalopods eject a cloud of darkly colored ink that confuses predators as the cephalopod makes a getaway. Cephalopods that live in dark places, such as vampire squids, eject glowing mucus blobs instead of darkly colored ink blobs. Glowing mucus blobs distract predators while a vampire squid escapes.

"e-jelly" in the ocean off the coast of Japan, about 3,000 feet (910 m) below the surface. The system worked; it attracted a giant squid's attention, and the animal came close enough for the Medusa camera to catch it on film.

About a week later, Kubodera and the team captured even more footage, this time nearly face-to-face with a giant squid from their seats on the *Triton* submersible. They'd brought down some bait hoping the giant squid would reveal itself, and, once again, it did. Despite this stunning footage from the 2012 expedition, humans have yet to witness a giant squid battling a sperm whale in the deep.

Humans have, however, made observations that lead scientists to believe these epic squid versus whale battles do take place. Sometimes, dead sperm whales wash ashore with scars that appear to be from a giant squid's suction-cupped arms. Scientists have also found large squid beaks inside dead whales' stomachs. From the size of the beak, scientists can estimate how big the squid was before it was eaten. Maybe someday you will be the first person to film a sperm whale trying to take down a giant squid.

Sea jellies, animals with jellylike bodies that lack hearts, brains, or blood, also live in the deep, dark places of the world, although they can also live in shallow places. Sea jellies can be as tiny as a pinprick or even longer than a whale. The lion's mane jelly has a bell that can grow to be 8 feet (almost 2½ m) across with tentacles that can grow longer than 100 feet (30 m).

Construct a Squid

Reuse a plastic bottle by constructing a squid, complete with jet propulsion. See if you can get your squid to jet all the way across a bathtub or a large storage bin filled with water. This activity requires access to a faucet or hose.

ADULT SUPERVISION REQUIRED

YOU'LL NEED

- 24-ounce (1½-pint) plastic bottle
- Scissors
- Hole punch
- Yarn
- Black permanent marker
- Medium or large balloon
- Bathtub or large storage bin

1. Cut off the top portion of a 24-ounce (1½-pint) plastic bottle, about 2 inches (5 cm) down from the cap. Remove the label from the bottle if you can.

2. Make four ½-inch-long (1¼-cm) slits near the base of the bottle and then widen each slit by cutting out a small piece of the bottle. These holes will come in handy later.

3. Punch 10 holes around the opening of the bottle using a hole punch.

4. Cut 10 pieces of yarn each 12 inches (30 cm) long and tie one into each hole. The yarn represents the squid's arms and tentacles.

5. Use a black permanent marker to draw two large eyes on either side of the plastic bottle near the arms.

6. Fill up a bathtub or a large bin with room-temperature water.

7. Fit the mouth of a balloon around a faucet or hose. Hold the water bottle so the balloon is as far down inside the bottle as you can get it, at least three-quarters of the way down is recommended.

8. Slowly turn on the faucet so the balloon begins to fill with water. When the balloon is just about full, turn off the faucet.

9. Pinch the neck of the balloon with one hand and carefully release the top of the balloon from the faucet. The water-filled balloon should press tightly against the bottle so the bottle doesn't need to be held in place anymore.

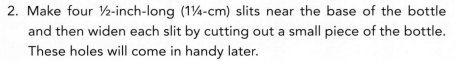

continued . . .

10. It's time to try out your squid's jet propulsion. Still pinching the neck of the balloon so the water doesn't escape, place the squid horizontally into the tub of water. Hold the squid near the bottom of the tub (it should be fully underwater) until all the air bubbles escape from the slits you made at the base of the bottle.

11. When there are no more air bubbles, release the balloon and watch what happens. Just like a real squid, the water stored in your squid's mantle cavity (the balloon) gets released through a siphon (the neck of the balloon), and the squid propels through the water.

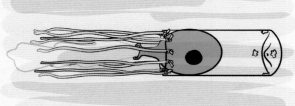

12. Fill the balloon a few more times to see if you can get your squid to jet all the way across the tub. Experiment with the way you fill the balloon and how full you make it.

Tip

If the squid pops up to the surface when you release the balloon, try making the slits at the base of the bottle larger. The more water you add to the balloon, the better your squid will jet.

Jellies have stinging tentacles that they use to defend themselves and to stun prey. Stings from some sea jellies can be painful to humans too. A sting from a box jelly, one of any square-shaped sea jelly relatives called cubozoans, can even be deadly thanks to its particularly powerful venom.

Siphonophores, another group of sea jelly relatives, include the venomous Portuguese man-of-war. A siphonophore is really a group of organisms that live together in a colony. Each organism in the colony has a special role and can't live on its own. If you could see a deep-sea siphonophore, such as the giant siphonophore, in its natural habitat, it would look like a glowing strings of lights suspended in blackness.

Life Finds a Way

Many deep-sea creatures, including siphonophores, sea jellies, squids, and deep-sea fish, give off "living light" called **bioluminescence**. Organisms with bioluminescence are bioluminescent. Some bioluminescent organisms have light-producing organs called photophores. Inside these organs, a chemical called luciferin reacts with oxygen to create light energy that gives off little or no heat.

Other organisms, such as flashlight fish, are bioluminescent thanks to their relationship with bioluminescent bacteria. A flashlight fish's light organs, which look like bean-shaped pouches beneath each eye, are packed with bioluminescent bacteria. Some flashlight fish create a blinking-light

Compose a Sea Monster Poem

Imagine being William Beebe on one of his first trips to the deep sea. If you saw something strange, it's likely you were the first person to see that strange thing! You'd need to describe it to your fellow scientists. Try to describe a pretend sea monster in the form of a poem. If you need inspiration, do an image search on the Internet for "deep-sea creature," and then check out Alfred Tennyson's poem "The Kraken."

YOU'LL NEED

🐟 Pen or pencil and paper or computer with word-processing software

Use your imagination to create a four-line poem that uses an *aabb* rhyme scheme.

In an *aabb* rhyme scheme, the last word of the first line rhymes with the last word of the second line and the last word of the third line rhymes with the last word of the fourth line.

Use this set of poetic instructions in *aabb* to help:

If sea monsters are scary, but inspire you to <u>think</u>, (a)
Then pick up a pen; your poem won't <u>stink</u>! (a)
Have fun and we promise, it'll all be <u>OK</u>. (b)
Writing and rhyming is a fun way to <u>play</u>! (b)

If you like writing poems, add four or even eight more lines. When you're done with your poem, read it aloud to a friend or family member.

"The Kraken" by Alfred Tennyson (1830)

Below the thunders of the upper deep,
Far, far beneath in the abysmal sea,
His ancient, dreamless, uninvaded sleep
The Kraken sleepeth: faintest sunlights flee
About his shadowy sides; above him swell
Huge sponges of millennial growth and height;
And far away into the sickly light,
From many a wondrous grot and secret cell
Unnumber'd and enormous polypi
Winnow with giant arms the slumbering green.
There hath he lain for ages, and will lie
Battening upon huge sea-worms in his sleep,
Until the latter fire shall heat the deep;
Then once by man and angels to be seen,
In roaring he shall rise and on the surface die.

Extra Credit

Up for a challenge? Try writing a sea monster sonnet. Research the rules of a sonnet first, but don't be afraid to break a few of the rules. (Tennyson did!)

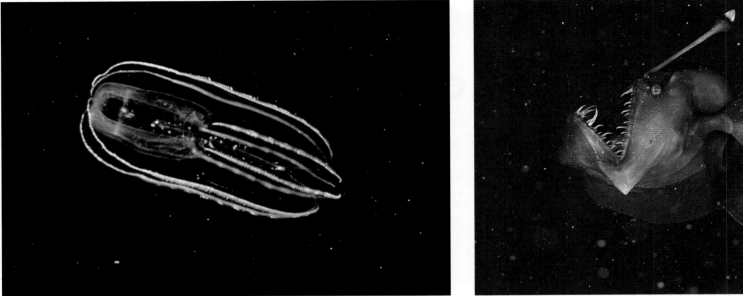

effect by covering or uncovering their illuminated photophores, as if they were turning a flashlight on and off.

Creatures of the deep use living light to help them communicate with each other, to attract mates, or, like vampire squids that eject bioluminescent mucus, to trick predators. Some creatures such as the female anglerfish use light to lure prey.

Female anglerfish have a strange fishing rod–like fin poking out of their foreheads. The tip of this bioluminescent rod glows. To attract prey, an anglerfish wiggles its lighted lure conveniently near its mouth. As soon as a curious fish comes close enough, the anglerfish strikes.

Bioluminescence can also help an animal blend in with its background. Similar to countershading (think back to the black-and-white Adélie penguins), **counterillumination** is a type of camouflage that

helps creatures better match their surroundings. Counterillumination works best where there is only a little bit of light.

Most creatures living in the ocean's dark midwaters have a row of small photophores along their undersides that they can use to match the amount of light around them. Because many deep-sea predators hunt by looking up—such as hatchetfish, which have eyes and jaws that permanently face up—these little lights help disguise an animal's shadow against a faintly lit background.

If the animal dives deeper, it can dim its lights to match the darker environment. If the animal swims up, it can brighten its lights to match the lighter environment. To get a better idea of how counterillumination works, complete the activity "Explore Marine Camouflage, Part 2: Who Glows There?" on the next page.

Explore Marine Camouflage, Part 2: Who Glows There?

Counterillumination is a type of camouflage that helps animals that live in dark places hide their silhouettes from predators and prey. This activity requires a darkened room.

YOU'LL NEED

- 2 sheets of black 12-by-12-inch (30-by-30-cm) cardstock
- Glow-in-the-dark paint (available at craft stores)
- Pencil
- Ruler (optional)
- Scissors
- Tape
- Flashlight

1. Begin by covering a sheet of black 12-by-12-inch (30-by-30-cm) cardstock with small dots of glow-in-the-dark paint. Paint at least 100 dots and be sure to cover the entire paper. If there are any big blank spots left when you're done, add some more dots.

2. Set this piece of cardstock aside to dry. It will be your background.

3. In the corner of a second piece of black cardstock (same size), use a pencil and a ruler, if needed, to draw the outline of a fish that's about 3 inches (7½ cm) tall by 6 inches (15 cm) long. Leave enough room on the cardstock for three more fish.

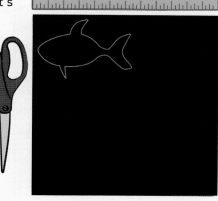

4. Cut out the fish shape.

5. Trace the fish three times and cut out the additional fish shapes.

6. Now that you have four fish, set two of them aside. The two you set aside represent animals that don't have counterillumination.

7. Add at least 30 glow-in-the-dark paint dots to each of the two remaining fish. These fish represent animals that have counterillumination. Set the two dotted fish aside to dry.

continued . . .

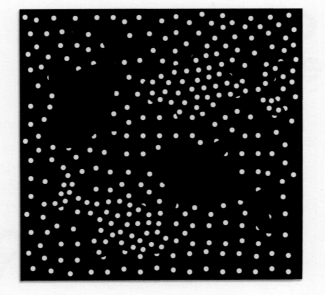

8. Once dry, tape all four fish to the background. Each fish should cover several paint dots. Tape your scene to a blank wall.

9. Shine a flashlight directly on the fish and the background for about a minute. Then turn off the lights to make the room dark.

10. As your eyes adjust, take a look at your glowing creation. How many fish shapes do you see? Which fish are easier to spot—the ones with counterillumination or the ones without it?

Extra Credit

How is counterillumination similar to and different from countershading, which you explored in "Explore Marine Camouflage, Part 1: Penguin Hide-and-Seek"? The two forms of camouflage accomplish the same goal in different ways. Why doesn't countershading work in the deep?

How do animals that live in the dark see? Compared to humans, some animal species, such as cats, have highly sensitive eyes that allow them to see without much light. In the deep, some creatures have large eyes relative to the size of their bodies that can take in more light. Giant squid eyes, for instance, can be as big as soccer balls! Other creatures have eyes shaped like tubes, which allows for large eyes even in small heads.

Animals in the deep must also live under pressure. Deep divers in the animal kingdom, such as sperm whales and elephant seals, have flexible skeletons that can collapse under the increasing pressure as they dive from the ocean's surface to its deeper layers. Animals that live their entire lives in the deep are well suited for this environment because the pressure inside their bodies matches the pressure outside of their bodies.

Mud Life

Compared to a tropical coral reef, life on the deep seafloor might seem pretty dull. Most creatures on the deep seafloor move slowly, grow slowly, and do everything they can to preserve energy. However, there are many interesting creatures that live down deep in the mud, including some that might seem familiar—invertebrates.

Invertebrates reign on the bottom of the ocean. There are sea stars called brittle stars, as well as deep-dwelling species of sea cucumbers, sea urchins, sea anemones, and even corals that don't require warm, sunlit waters to survive.

These deep-sea invertebrates are similar to their relatives in shallower waters; they've just adapted to conditions at the bottom.

Bottom-dwelling fish must also adapt to the deep-sea environment. Tripod fish have learned how to hunt without wasting too much precious energy. A tripod fish faces the current and perches on its three long fins as it waits for food to drift by.

Ratfish are other bottom dwellers that have skeletons made of cartilage like their shark and ray cousins. Also like sharks and rays, ratfish have a powerful sense of smell and can detect electric fields. These senses help a ratfish find food such as worms and crabs buried in the muddy seafloor.

Large, pale crustaceans called giant isopods also creep in the deep mud. Known to grow to be more than a foot (30 cm) in length, giant isopods have strong exoskeletons that help protect them from predators. Similar to pill bugs or "roly-polies" you might find on the sidewalk, giant isopods can curl themselves into a ball when threatened.

Because food can be scarce in the deep, giant isopods can slow their heartbeat to use less energy. Using this strategy, giant isopods can survive without eating, if needed, for years. When a food source finally does come along, giant isopods gorge themselves to make up for lost time.

Deep-Sea Communities

Every once in a while, a humongous gift in the form of a dead whale drifts down from above and lands on the seafloor. When this happens,

(left) **Brittle stars are a group of sea stars that can live in very deep places.** *NOAA Okeanos Explorer Program, INDEX-SATAL 2010*

(center) **A tripod fish perches on the seafloor.** *NOAA Okeanos Explorer Program, INDEX-SATAL 2010, NOAA/OER*

(right) **Giant isopods are basically deep-sea versions of roly-polies.** *NOAA Expedition to the Deep Slope 2006*

(left) **A whale fall provides a feast for deep-sea creatures that can last for several years.** *Courtesy of Craig Smith, University of Hawaii*

(right) **The top of a chimney formed by minerals pluming from a vent in the seafloor.** *Submarine Ring of Fire 2004 Exploration, NOAA Vents Program*

creatures from all around come to enjoy the banquet. The carcass, and the community that gathers around it, is called a whale fall.

Whale falls are an important part of the deep-sea ecosystem. Since there isn't much spare food in the deep, when a 100-ton piece of meat plops down in the mud, it's a big deal for the hundreds of creatures that will feast on the whale for the next several years.

When a whale carcass first falls, it still has soft tissue attached to the bone. This first phase of a whale fall attracts **scavengers** such as crabs, hagfish, and sleeper sharks like the Pacific sleeper. Once the soft tissue is gone, worms, snails, and shrimps move in to pick at the leftovers. In the final stage of a whale fall, bacteria finish off what's left of the whale. These bacteria cover the remaining carcass, making it look fuzzy like a mat or rug.

In 1977, a crew of geologists dove more than a mile (1.6 km) down in the Atlantic Ocean inside a Woods Hole Oceanographic Institution submersible called *Alvin*. Their goal was to explore an ocean ridge near the Galápagos Islands. The research crew ended up making an exciting discovery—a deep-sea community surrounding hot water vents.

As the seafloor shifts and spreads, **hydrothermal vents** form when seawater pours through cracks in the Earth's crust and comes in contact with hot melted rocks called magma. There, the seawater heats up like water in a teakettle, except much hotter, reaching 700 degrees Fahrenheit (370 degrees Celsius) or more. The water becomes so hot that it shoots back up through the vent and into the ocean, bringing minerals and chemicals from the Earth's core with it.

As the hydrothermal vent fluid cools back down, it dumps some of those minerals around the vent opening. These minerals pile up and form structures that look like chimneys. One such chimney was nicknamed Godzilla because it grew so tall—nearly 15 stories high. Eventually, Godzilla became too tall; it collapsed under its own weight.

Sometimes, the plume from a vent chimney looks like black smoke because the hydrothermal vent fluid is rich in dark-colored minerals. Scientists call these vents "black smokers." When the hydrothermal vent fluid is rich in light-colored minerals, it looks like there's white smoke coming from the chimney. Scientists call these vents "white smokers."

As the *Alvin* crew discovered in 1977, communities of deep-sea organisms live in the hot, chemical-filled environments surrounding hydrothermal vents. White clams the size of dinner plates, squat lobsters and yeti crabs, and vent tubeworms are just a few of the unique creatures that thrive there.

Vent tubeworms are fast-growing, deep-sea worms encased in long tubes that grow straight up out of the seafloor. At the end of the white tubes are red, feathery plumes. Like an exoskeleton, the tube's hard casing protects the worm inside from predators and toxic chemicals coming from the vents. On a return expedition in 1979, a team of biologists aboard *Alvin* discovered a new vent site full of tubeworms. Since the strange worms and their tubes look like long-stemmed roses, they named the site Rose Garden.

The discovery of so much life in vent communities led scientists to ask new questions. While most ecosystems rely on plants that generate energy from sunlight, hydrothermal vent communities thrive at the bottom of the ocean where there is no sunlight at all. Where were these creatures getting the energy they needed to survive?

The fluid billowing out of hydrothermal vents is filled with chemicals such as hydrogen sulfide, a toxic gas that smells like rotten eggs. Similar to the way phytoplankton turns sunlight into energy through photosynthesis near the surface, microscopic organisms called microbes turn chemicals into energy through a process called **chemosynthesis**.

Vent tubeworms are deep-sea worms that live near hydrothermal vents. *NOAA Okeanos Explorer Program, Galapagos Rift Expedition 2011*

Deep-Sea Bologna Sandwiches

About a decade before the team of geologists discovered hydrothermal vent communities aboard the *Alvin* deep-sea submersible, *Alvin* sank. In October 1968, shortly after crewmembers aboard *Alvin* were lowered into the Atlantic Ocean to begin an underwater research expedition, two steel cables snapped, and the submersible began to sink. The crew escaped, but *Alvin* came to rest 5,000 feet (over 1,500 m) down on the bottom of the ocean.

Nearly a year later, a recovery mission succeeded in bringing *Alvin* back up to the surface. Even though it had sunk, *Alvin*'s time at the bottom of the sea would still prove valuable to the scientific community. The crew's lunches, including apples and bologna sandwiches, were still inside, and they were strangely well preserved. Besides being a bit soggy and discolored, the food seemed nearly as fresh as it had on the day the crew packed their lunches.

This discovery made scientists curious. How could fruit and bologna survive for so long without decaying? An apple or a bologna sandwich certainly wouldn't have fared so well if it had been sitting on a kitchen counter for a year, or even if it had been in the fridge for the same amount of time. There must be something about the conditions of the deep sea that left year-old bologna sandwiches "soggy but edible."

As it turns out, the high pressure, cold temperatures, and lack of oxygen 5,000 feet down all contributed to the bologna miracle. This combination of conditions slowed the growth of microbes that normally cause food to decay. Because most kitchens aren't under as much pressure as the deep sea, nor are they freezing cold or lacking in oxygen, year-old bologna sandwiches left on the counter wouldn't be nearly as exciting—or as edible—as the *Alvin* deep-sea sandwiches.

Clams, mussels, snails, and shrimps in vent communities eat these microbes. Fish and other deep-sea predators eat the clams, mussels, snails, and shrimps, and the food chain continues on. Some vent creatures, such as tubeworms, get energy by hosting microbes within their bodies (similar to the way coral polyps host algae). Tubeworms give microbes a place to live in exchange for energy and nutrients.

Cold seeps are areas of the ocean floor where chemicals such as methane bubble up from cracks in the Earth's crust. Chemosynthesis supports life in these areas too. Unlike hot hydrothermal vent communities, cold seeps are the same temperature as the surrounding water. Chimneys don't form around cold seeps.

While the creatures that live around hydrothermal vents tend to grow quickly, cold seep communities are full of long-living, slower-growing species of mussels, worms, and crabs. Scientists believe cold-seep worms may live for more than 250 years.

Occasionally, life congregates around something unnatural that has landed on the seafloor, such as a shipwreck. Shipwrecks are scattered across the bottom of the ocean in both deep places and shallow places. As ships sink, they often break apart and create a wide field of debris along the seafloor. When cargo ships, passenger ships, war ships, submarines, and airplanes sink to the bottom, they become home to a vast number of creatures such as corals, sea anemones, worms, crabs, and fish. In some instances, scientists have sunk

ships on purpose to form artificial reef communities that become sanctuaries for marine life.

Shipwrecks are fascinating places humans like to write about, sing songs about, and tell ghost stories about. Some wrecks, such as the *Andrea Doria*, a 697-foot (212½-m) Italian passenger liner that sunk in 1956 after a collision with another ship, are just within reach of experienced scuba divers at about 250 feet (76 m). Other wrecks, such as the *Titanic*, an 883-foot (269-m) British liner that sank in 1912 after striking an iceberg, are so deep that they can only be explored by submersible. Today, the *Titanic* rests beneath more than 12,000 feet (almost 3,660 m) of water off the coast of Newfoundland.

Shipwrecks are common in large lakes such as North America's Lake Michigan, which has more than 350 wreck sites. Humans can usually access these wrecks because lakes aren't nearly as deep as the ocean, though they can be quite deep.

So far this book has focused on ecosystems and life in the ocean. However, you're about to travel inland. About 3 percent of Earth's water is not salty seawater; it's **freshwater** that can be found in rivers, streams, lakes, and ponds.

Some deep-sea creatures have large eyes relative to the size of their bodies. *NOAA Okeanos Explorer Program, Our Deepwater Backyard: Exploring Atlantic Canyons and Seamounts*

Rivers, Streams, Lakes, and Ponds

5

I am born high up in the mountains. As snow melts, it feeds me. When it rains, I swell and grow. I flow down the mountain, carving a path for myself as I go. More water finds me from the left and the right; it joins me on my journey to the sea. When there's an obstacle, I overcome it. I tumble over rocks and fall hundreds of feet before starting again. I bend this way and that way; I fork and branch off, but gravity keeps me going.

I support plants and animals—both big and small. Entire ecosystems depend on me. Each year, I am a witness as millions of fish and insects are born, as tadpoles transform into frogs, as beavers build homes, as bears and moose come to feed at my banks, and as salmon insist on swimming the wrong way.

Eventually I reach the ocean. I slow down, spread out, and dump whatever I'm carrying into the big blue sea. But my story doesn't end there. Back up on the mountain, I'm still flowing. Can you guess what I am?

If you guessed that I'm a river, you're correct. This is the pretend life story of a river fed by snowmelt and

A river runs through Torres del Paine National Park in Chile.
Courtesy of Bruce Fryxell

rainwater in the mountains. Each river has its own story. Some dry up after just one season, while others keep flowing year after year. Rivers are also part of Earth's story. They have changed the planet by carving majestic valleys and canyons into the landscape.

Rivers are important to humans. Throughout history, rivers have provided the water humans need for drinking and growing crops. They've also provided a way to transport goods, people, and ideas from place to place. Many ancient civilizations rose, fell, and rebuilt again along the banks of rivers. Many of the same rivers support some of today's greatest cities.

The water in most rivers, streams, lakes, and ponds is part of Earth's supply of freshwater. Compared to seawater, freshwater is not salty. Almost 70 percent of Earth's freshwater exists as ice, especially **glaciers** and the large sheets of glacial ice that cover Antarctica and Greenland. The rest of Earth's freshwater exists as groundwater (water stored underground in the soil and the spaces between broken rock) or as surface water in lakes and other freshwater systems.

Freshwater Systems

None of the water coming out of your sink faucet, falling from the sky as rain, or flowing in a river is new. Earth's supply of freshwater is part of a never-ending process called the water cycle.

Hang a wet beach towel in the sun, and you'll witness the first step of the water cycle: evaporation, the change of liquid water into a gas. As the sun warms the water molecules on the surface of the towel, the molecules heat up to the point of becoming vapor that rises into Earth's **atmosphere**. As the water evaporates from the towel, the towel dries.

The temperature is cooler in the atmosphere than it is on Earth's surface, so water that evaporates from rivers, lakes, and the ocean cools as it rises. As it cools, the water vapor turns back into a liquid. This is called condensation. If you've ever noticed a glass of cool lemonade sweating in the summer heat, you've witnessed condensation firsthand. When water vapor in the surrounding air touches the cool glass, it condenses on the outside of the glass, forming drops of liquid water.

Clouds form when water vapor condenses on tiny particles in the atmosphere. As more water condenses inside the cloud, water droplets join together and get heavier. When they become too heavy, the water droplets fall to the ground as raindrops—this process is called precipitation. When conditions are right, precipitation can also mean snow, hail, or sleet.

After falling back to the surface of the Earth as precipitation, some of the water soaks into the soil. The rest flows from the land into rivers and streams, collecting in lakes, ponds, and the ocean. From there, evaporation starts the water cycle all over again.

After it rains, the rainwater flows into a river or a river system that drains into a lake or the ocean. A river system often includes smaller rivers and streams called tributaries, which deliver water from the surrounding land into the main river.

Transform Salt Water into Freshwater

If you start out with salt water, can the energy from the sun transform it into freshwater? Find out by using household items to create a miniature water cycle. This activity requires access to a sunny spot.

YOU'LL NEED

- 2 tablespoons of salt
- Food coloring (any color)
- 2 cups of warm water
- Large glass mixing bowl
- Small drinking glass or other container, such as a ramekin (the container must be shorter than the large glass mixing bowl)
- Plastic wrap
- Tape
- Small stone

1. Add 2 tablespoons of salt and two drops of food coloring to 2 cups of warm water. Stir the ingredients together until the salt dissolves completely. Dip your finger in the water and then touch the tip of your tongue. How does the water taste?

2. Pour the salty water into a large glass mixing bowl.

3. Place a small container in the center of the mixing bowl. The container should be heavy enough to displace the water and sit on the bottom. In other words, it should not float. The container should also be tall enough that water doesn't pour into it. If it does, find a different container or remove some of the water from the large mixing bowl.

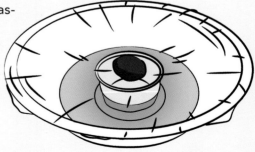

4. Cover the mixing bowl with plastic wrap and press the edges down to seal it. The plastic should have a little bit of slack in the middle, but there shouldn't be any gaps around the edges. Tape the edges of the plastic down in a few places to make sure it stays in place.

5. Place a small stone on the plastic directly above the small container so it creates a depression in the plastic.

6. Bring your bowl outside and place it in the sun.

continued . . .

7. After about three hours, check on your bowl. Gently tap the stone to encourage the drops of condensation to drip into the small container.

8. After another hour or two, check on the bowl again. Tap the stone to get more condensation to drip into the small container.

9. Remove the stone and the plastic and take out the small container. What color is the water inside? Dip your finger into the water and taste it. How does it compare to the water in the larger bowl?

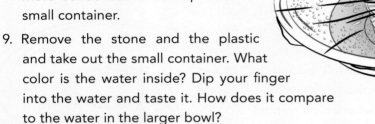

Extra Credit

Draw a diagram of the miniature water cycle that just happened in your bowl. Label the following processes on your diagram: evaporation, condensation, and precipitation.

The area of land drained by a particular river system is called a drainage basin or watershed. The Amazon River and its many tributaries drain the largest watershed in the world—more than 2 million square miles (5.2 million km²) of land in South America.

Lakes, bodies of water surrounded by land, form when water collects in a low part of the landscape. Lakes come in all sizes; some are shallow, some are deep, some are narrow enough to swim across, and some are so wide that they look like an ocean. If you're standing in Chicago, Illinois, on the shore of Lake Michigan, you won't be able to wave hi to someone across the lake in Indiana or Michigan, because the lake is simply too big to see to the other side.

Many plants and animals rely on babbling brooks, meandering streams, raging rivers, tiny ponds, and awe-inspiring lakes for survival. From baby insects and baby fish to hippos and crocodiles, freshwater ecosystems are full of life.

Freshwater Life

Many insects, including species within the dragonfly, mayfly, mosquito, and water beetle families, live in and around freshwater habitats. In some cases, these insects live completely underwater during the first stage of their lives.

Mayflies lay their eggs in the still waters of lakes and ponds. When mayfly **nymphs** hatch, they eat algae and continue to live in the water as they grow, shed their skin, and develop wings. After taking on a winged form, the mayflies leave the water and take flight. They shed their skin a final time, taking on their fully adult form. Adult mayflies live out the rest of their short lives in the air surrounding a freshwater habitat. Sometimes in a matter of hours, they mate, lay their eggs (if female), and then die.

Insects in all stages of their life cycles are an important food source for freshwater fish. Trout are common freshwater fish that eat insects, as well as crustaceans and smaller fish. Catfish have whisker-like barbels on the sides of their mouths that they use to find insects and other prey, often at the muddy bottoms of rivers and lakes.

Most fish have gills and a separate oxygen-filled organ called a swim bladder. Swim bladders help fish stay at the same depth without rising or sinking. Fish called lungfish, which live in rivers and lakes in Africa, Australia, and South America, have gills, but they also have modified swim bladders that act like lungs by allowing the fish to breathe air. To do so, a lungfish swims to the surface and sticks the tip of its snout out just enough to suck in some air before a predator, such as a shoebill stork, takes notice.

Besides fish and insects, freshwater ecosystems also support frogs and toads, as well as newts and other salamanders. This group of animals—amphibians—often lives partly on land and partly in the water. The word *amphibian* comes from the Greek word *amphibios*, which means "living a double life."

Amphibians undergo **metamorphosis**, a major change in an animal's form after birth; this often includes moving from water to land. Similar to

a butterfly's transformation from a crawling caterpillar to a flying adult butterfly, an amphibian such as a frog transforms from a swimming tadpole to a land-dwelling adult.

Frogs start their life cycle as eggs, which are often laid in a large group underwater. When it's time to hatch, tadpoles (baby frogs) emerge. Tadpoles have gills to absorb oxygen underwater and tails for swimming.

As the tadpoles eat and grow, legs start to appear, lungs develop to replace gills, and tails get smaller and smaller as limbs grow. Once properly equipped for life on land, the frogs leave the water, though most return to freshwater to mate and lay eggs.

You may also find turtles in freshwater ecosystems. Some freshwater turtles spend most of their lives in water, while others split their time more

Many amphibians begin their lives in the water and then spend much of their adult lives on land. *Courtesy of Mark Gonka*

Fold an Origami Frog

Now that you've learned about amphibians, make one of your own. All you need is some patience and a piece of paper. Follow along with the photos to fold an origami frog.

YOU'LL NEED

- 8½-by-11-inch sheet of printer paper
- Markers, crayons, or colored pencils (optional)

1. Place the sheet of paper on a table with the short edge at the top.
2. Bring the top-left corner to the right edge of the paper, and make a fold line starting at the top-right corner. (A)
3. Unfold the paper. (B)
4. Repeat in the other direction. Bring the top-right corner to the left edge of the paper, and make a fold line starting at the top-left corner. (C)
5. Unfold the paper. Your fold lines should make an X. (D)
6. Flip the paper over and fold the top of the paper down to create a new crease that runs horizontally through the center of the X-shaped fold lines. (E)
7. Unfold the paper and flip it back over. (F)
8. Place one finger on each side of the new crease and pull the creases together and down, forming a triangle on top of a rectangle. (G–I)
9. Fold the left corner of the triangle up to meet the top of the triangle. (J)

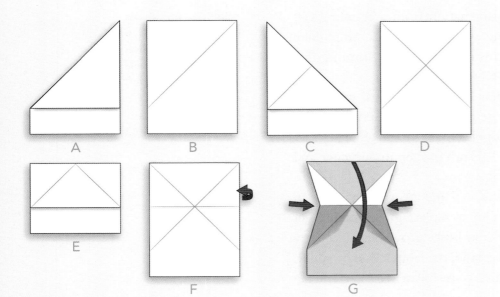

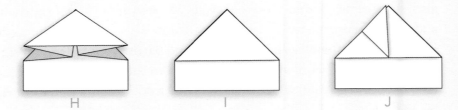

10. Fold the right corner of the triangle up to the meet the top of the triangle. (K)

11. Fold both sides of the bottom rectangle in to meet each other in the center. (L)

12. Fold the bottom of the lower square up to the middle of the diamond shape. (M)

13. Fold the bottom rectangle in half by bringing the top edge to the bottom. (N)

14. Flip over your frog and admire your creation! If you'd like, decorate your origami by coloring it green and adding eyes and other features.

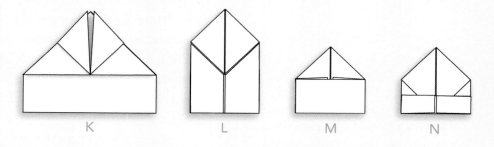

K   L   M   N

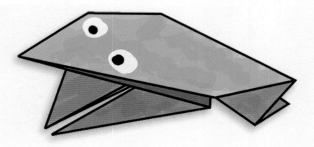

Extra Credit

Use the Internet to find instructions for how to make an origami tadpole. Once you have an origami tadpole and an origami frog, write a paragraph about how a tadpole transforms into a frog as it undergoes metamorphosis.

evenly between water and land. When it's time to lay their eggs, freshwater turtles choose a spot on land near the water, dig a hole, lay their eggs, and leave. When the baby turtles hatch, they must find their way to the water on their own.

Most turtles have thick, overlapping scales called scutes, which shield their backs from predators. Some freshwater species, known as softshells, and one marine species, the leatherback sea turtle, have shells covered by leathery skin instead of rigid scutes. Softshell turtles' lightweight shells help them move quickly, both in water and on land.

Some freshwater turtles munch on plants and insects that live in and around the water, while others are hunters. Snapping turtles are predators that hunt frogs, fish, snakes, and other small animals. Alligator snapping turtles have a small worm-like piece of flesh on their tongues that they use as a lure to attract prey.

Other predators in freshwater ecosystems include birds and mammals. Birds feed on the fish and insects that live in, on, and around the water. Mammals in a freshwater habitat might live in the water, such as river dolphins; they might live partially in the water and partially out of the water, like beavers; or they might be land dwellers that come to the water to feed, like moose and bears.

Each year at Brooks Falls in Alaska's Katmai National Park, brown bears come to feed on sockeye salmon as the fish swim up Brooks River to **spawn**. Like other species of Pacific salmon, sockeye salmon are born in freshwater and then migrate to the ocean, where they spend their adult lives.

When it's time to reproduce, sockeye salmon return to the river in which they were born. To reach the spawning grounds, groups of salmon swim against the current, sometimes leaping into the air to clear obstacles as they travel upstream. As they leap, brown bears are there to catch them.

The type of wildlife that can be found in a freshwater ecosystem depends on where in the world it is located. For instance, you wouldn't find the same creatures in North America's Lake Superior that you'd find in Africa's Nile River. Let's take a closer look at some of the world's freshwater ecosystems.

Predators in freshwater ecosystems may include large mammals, like brown bears. *Courtesy of Lisa Hupp*

Catch the Salmon! Tag Game

Brown bears in Alaska's Katmai National Park come to the river to catch salmon as the fish migrate upstream to spawn. Pretend you're a brown bear or a salmon as you play a marine science version of tag. This activity requires a large outdoor space and a group of at least six people.

Objective

If you're a bear, try to catch (tag) as many salmon as possible as they travel upstream to the spawning grounds. If you're a salmon, try to reach the spawning grounds without being "eaten" by bears!

Setup

Choose two players to be the brown bears. The remaining players will be salmon.

As a group, define the area of play by setting up boundaries that no one will be able to cross.

Select an area on one side of the playing field to be a safe zone—the "spawning grounds." The safe zone could be a tree, a rock, or a circle you draw in the dirt. When the salmon reach the spawning grounds, they are safe and can no longer be tagged.

Decide on a boundary line somewhere in the middle of the playing field. The boundary line represents a small waterfall. Bears can't pass this line, and salmon have to jump over the waterfall to cross it.

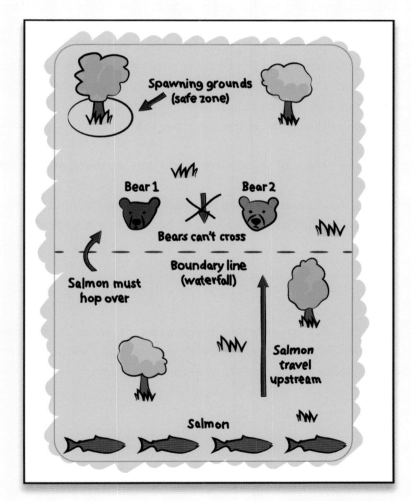

continued . . .

How to Play

To start, the bears stand "upstream" on the same side of the field as the spawning grounds. The salmon stand on the opposite side of the field as far "downstream" as possible without going out of bounds.

Count down as a group—"Five, four, three, two, one—GO!"

Salmon must try to get past the bears to the spawning grounds without being tagged. If a salmon is tagged, he/she must sit out of bounds until the next round.

Salmon can run, but they must hop over the waterfall.

Bears try to tag the salmon as the fish cross the waterfall to get to the spawning grounds.

The game ends when all salmon are either safe at the spawning grounds or eaten.

When the first round ends, choose two new bears for the next round. Continue playing until everyone has had the chance to be a bear and a salmon.

Tip

Mix up game-play by selecting more bears or fewer bears, creating obstacles salmon need to overcome at the boundary line, or having the salmon run backward to simulate swimming upstream.

Mighty Rivers

The Amazon River is a mighty river indeed. It flows about 4,000 miles (almost 6,500 km) across South America, from the Andes Mountains in Peru to the Atlantic Ocean. Within its waters are a vast number of species, including one of the largest freshwater fish in the world, the arapaima, which can be 8 feet (almost 2½ m) long or more—bigger than a human! Similar to the lungfish, the arapaima is an air-breathing fish that comes to the surface for oxygen. When it takes a gulp of air, the fish makes a funny noise that sounds like a grunt or a cough.

Another unique fish living in the Amazon River is the piranha. Piranhas have sharp triangle-shaped teeth, strong jaws, and a bad reputation for being vicious predators. Red-bellied piranhas often live together in groups. Though they prefer to scavenge on worms, insects, and small fish, piranhas occasionally take down larger animals. If a group of hungry piranhas comes across a small mammal that's sick or injured, the fish might engage in a feeding frenzy by zooming in to bite off chunks of the animal's flesh.

Other creatures living in and around the Amazon River include large rodents called capybaras, giant river otters, water-loving snakes called anacondas, and Amazon river dolphins, which have pinkish-gray skin. Surrounding the Amazon River is one of the most diverse ecosystems on the planet—the Amazon rain forest, which is home to several species of monkeys, parrots, poison dart frogs, sloths, bats, and more.

A little more than 4,100 miles (about 6,600 km) long, the Nile River is the longest river in the world. It flows northward from its main source, Lake Victoria, through several African countries into Egypt, and then drains into the Mediterranean Sea. The Nile River system is home to many species of fish, including catfish, lungfish, and eels. The huge Nile perch, which can weigh more than 400 pounds (180 kg), also swims in these waters.

Besides fish, the greater Nile River system is home to other animals such as the hippopotamus. These massive mammals love to keep cool in rivers and lakes, leaving only at night to graze on grass. Hippos even sleep in the water! However, hippo herds with young calves must always keep a watchful eye out for predators, such as the Nile crocodile.

Nile crocodiles can be 16 feet (almost 5 m) long, sometimes even longer. While these crocs eat mostly fish, their powerful jaws make it possible to take down much larger prey, such as zebras and young hippos. A croc's body shape is perfect for seeing without being seen; it might lurk in the water with just its eyes, ears, and nostrils poking out above the surface. When they lurk in the water or lie still on land, crocodiles look like harmless logs.

Despite being powerful, even deadly, crocodiles are devoted parents. Unlike most reptiles that lay their eggs and leave, crocs guard their nests until the eggs hatch and then protect their young from predators for some time after birth.

The Chinese alligator lives in another one of Earth's mighty rivers—the Yangtze, which flows

(left) **Hippos spend most of their time in the water, leaving at night to graze.** *Courtesy of Bruce Fryxell*

(right) **How many crocs do you count?** *Courtesy of Mark Gonka*

Call Me Croc or Call Me Gator?

All alligators are crocodilians, but not all crocodilians are alligators. Confused? Don't be. Alligators and crocodiles are part of a group of animals called crocodilians. Within this group, alligators are in one family and crocodiles are in another family.

Crocs and gators are large reptiles with long bodies covered with scales and bony plates. They have muscular tails, four short legs, and webbed toes with claws, but there are some ways to tell them apart. If the animal has a long, narrow jaw that's pointed like a *V*, it's

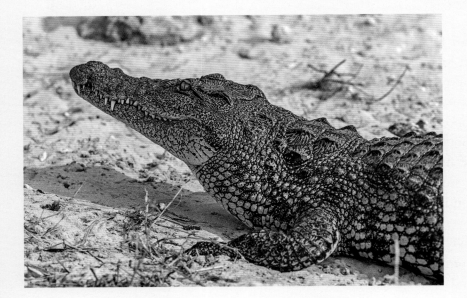

probably a crocodile. If the animal has a shorter, *U*-shaped snout, it's probably an alligator. Alligators' *U*-shaped snouts are particularly helpful for breaking the hard shells of turtles and invertebrates.

Which teeth poke out when the animal closes its mouth? An alligator's upper jaw is a bit larger than its lower jaw, so when it closes its mouth, its bottom teeth fit inside and aren't visible. A crocodile's upper and lower jaws are about the same size. Therefore, when a croc closes its mouth, its upper and lower teeth stick out and the croc's grin appears quite toothy.

For the most part, alligators and crocodiles live in different places. Alligators stick to lakes, rivers, and freshwater swamps in the southeastern United States (North America) and near the Yangtze River in China (Asia). Crocodiles can tolerate salt water, so they're found in more habitats, including somewhat salty environments like mangrove forests, and on more continents—Africa, Asia, North and South America, and Australia. Florida, a state in the southeastern United States, is the only place in the world where crocs and gators both live.

When a croc closes its mouth, its upper and lower teeth stick out.
Courtesy of Bruce Fryxell

Learn more about what you and your family can do to prevent species extinction in chapter 7.

3,900 miles (6,280 km) across China and empties into the East China Sea. The Chinese alligator is one of several endangered species that can be found within the vast Yangtze River basin. Others include the Chinese giant salamander, the Chinese pangolin, the snow leopard, and the giant panda, which lives in bamboo forests high up in the mountains surrounding the upper Yangtze.

The endangered Yangtze finless porpoise also lives here. Unlike most other cetaceans, these unique freshwater mammals don't have a dorsal fin. A freshwater mammal called the baiji dolphin once shared the Yangtze's waters but is now believed to be extinct. If humans don't change the way they interact with the Yangtze River and its wildlife, the Yangtze finless porpoise and many other endangered species could face the same reality.

In North America, the Colorado River starts in the Rocky Mountains, flowing southwest through parts of Wyoming, Colorado, Utah, Nevada, New Mexico, California, Arizona, and northwestern Mexico, where it empties into the Gulf of California. Along the way, the river flows through all kinds of habitats, from forest to desert.

Many animals call the Colorado River basin home, including the endangered humpback chub,

Horseshoe Bend, a feature of the Colorado River in Arizona.
Courtesy of Mark Gonka

a silvery fish with a fleshy hump behind its head. Humpback chubs live in the stretch of the river that flows through the Grand Canyon in northern Arizona. Large mammals such as bighorn sheep and mountain lions and smaller mammals such as beavers also rely on the Colorado River and its tributaries for food, water, or shelter.

Beavers are rodents with large front teeth that are strong enough to chew through wood. They have webbed hind feet to propel them through the water and flat, paddle-like tails to help them steer while swimming. A beaver's naturally oily fur repels water and keeps its skin dry, even while it's underwater.

Surviving in Icy Waters

What happens when a lake or a pond freezes over? Can the animals that live in the water survive? Yes! Here's why. As the air temperature above the lake drops, the water temperature at the surface of the lake gets colder too. As the surface water gets colder, it sinks because it becomes denser than the warmer water below it. Warmer water replaces the cold water at the surface. The new surface water gets colder as it's exposed to the air, until it's also dense enough to sink, and this happens again and again. After a while, the lake water is all the same temperature—about 39.2 degrees Fahrenheit (4 degrees Celsius).

Next, the water at the surface begins to freeze. Water becomes denser as it gets colder only until it hits 39.2 degrees Fahrenheit. Once the water temperature drops below this point, it begins to expand and become less dense. Therefore, when all the water is at 39.2 degrees, the surface water no longer sinks; it just freezes into an ice layer that floats on the top of the lake. The ice layer holds some heat and oxygen in the lake, creating perfectly acceptable conditions for fish and other organisms to survive in the waters below. Many animals lower their metabolic rate, the rate at which they use energy, during the winter. This helps them use less oxygen and survive with less food.

If ponds and lakes freeze over in the winter, why doesn't the ocean? Salt lowers the freezing point of water, so seawater needs to be much colder than freshwater to freeze. While many fish can survive in the 39.2-degree water below a frozen lake, their blood would freeze in water that drops too far below freezing point (32 degrees Fahrenheit, or 0 degrees Celsius).

When seawater temperatures drop too low, ocean fish must move to warmer waters or rely on special adaptations to survive. Some species produce an antifreeze molecule called glycoprotein, which stops their insides from freezing in extremely cold seawater.

Beavers use logs, tree branches, and mud to build dome-shaped shelters called lodges along the banks of a river. They often build **dams** to block streams and create ponds, deepening the water around their lodges. To further protect their homes from predators, beavers build secret underwater tunnel entrances.

Lake Communities

Freshwater systems often include lakes. Lakes may not be as big or as deep as the ocean, but many lakes are big enough to hold secrets. For centuries, humans have wondered whether a lake in Scotland called Loch Ness is home to a sea creature called Nessie, the Loch Ness monster. While some people claim to have seen Nessie, there is no scientific evidence that she exists (or ever existed) in this murky lake, which is more than 700 feet (210 m) deep.

Russia's Lake Baikal, nicknamed the Pearl of Siberia, reaches depths of more than 5,000 feet (1,500 m). Its waters are home to many animals that are unique to the lake, such as the Baikal seal, a freshwater relative of the Arctic ringed seal, which lives in the Arctic Ocean. The Baikal seal is the only seal species on Earth that spends its entire life in freshwater.

The Great Lakes, a string of five lakes on the border of the United States and Canada in North America, make up another one of the most impressive freshwater systems on Earth. Lakes Huron, **Ontario**, **Michigan**, Erie, and **Superior** (use the

acronym HOMES to remember their names) support many freshwater fish, such as lake whitefish, walleye, muskellunge, and lake trout. The Great Lakes system also supports mammals that come to eat and drink, including the gray wolf, the Canada lynx, and the bald eagle.

Not all lakes qualify as freshwater ecosystems; some lakes, like the Great Salt Lake in Utah, are salty. Rivers feed water and dissolved minerals into the Great Salt Lake, but there's nowhere for the water to go because the lake doesn't have an outlet to the sea. As water evaporates from the lake's surface, dissolved minerals such as salt are left behind. This leaves the lake water salty—saltier than the ocean, in fact. The Great Salt Lake is too salty for fish, but brine shrimp can live there.

The Dead Sea is a salty lake bordering Israel, the West Bank, and Jordan in the Middle East. The Jordan River feeds into the lake, but nothing flows out. Humans visit the Dead Sea from all around the world to float in its mineral-rich water. Because salty water is so dense, humans float like buoys on the surface of the lake. Microbes can live in the Dead Sea, but other life forms can't. However, fish and other organisms can live in the freshwater pools and streams surrounding the lake.

In fact, one reason lakes, ponds, rivers, and streams are so important is they support the ecosystems around them. **Wetland** ecosystems, such as marshes, bogs, and swamps, often form in low-lying areas surrounding rivers and lakes. Wetlands like mangrove forests may also form near coasts, which means wetlands may contain salt water, freshwater, or a mixture of both.

Wetlands of all types are important to humans because these areas collect, store, and filter water, preventing floods and helping to provide clean drinking water. Sadly, human activities are harming wetlands faster than the lands can recover. An important part of marine science is learning about how humans have affected ecosystems for better and for worse. As a marine scientist in training, it is part of your mission to help protect these natural places from harm.

Our Connected Earth

6

Sometimes, ecosystems get sick. Think of how your own body reacts when something new—such as a virus—is added to your system, or if something your body needs is taken away. In both cases, you get sick. If something new is added to an ecosystem that doesn't belong there, or if something is taken away, that ecosystem can also become unhealthy.

About 100 years ago, the giant kelp forests (underwater forests of tall seaweeds) near Monterey Bay, California, were sick. What was once a diverse coastal community supporting many fish, invertebrates, marine mammals, and seabirds, was now nearly gone. Monterey Bay's ecosystem was missing something important—something it depended on to be healthy, something that also happened to have incredibly soft fur.

Southern sea otters' dense fur helps keep them warm in cold water. Humans figured out a long time ago that fur could also keep *us* warm during cold winters. During the 18th and 19th centuries, humans began killing otters and selling their luxurious fur as

Southern sea otters were nearly hunted to extinction for their soft fur.
NOAA

part of the fur trade, the industry of buying and selling of animal fur. In some parts of the world, wearing sea otter fur was fashionable. Wealthy people paid a good deal of money for this "golden fleece," which was also sometimes called "soft gold."

By the early 1900s, southern sea otters were believed to be extinct in California. This was bad news for the kelp forests in the area. Without sea otters' constant snacking on sea urchins, the urchins ate the kelp faster than the kelp could grow back. Without kelp, there could be no kelp forest. Without a kelp forest, many native species were forced to move away or face death.

The story does get better. In 1938, a small colony of about 50 southern sea otters was discovered in a remote area along California's Big Sur coast. They hadn't gone extinct after all! Humans were beginning to understand that otters have more to offer than their fur; they are the caretakers of their marine ecosystems.

With the help of laws that made it illegal to hunt and kill southern sea otters and other endangered species, the otters that survived the fur trade years multiplied and spread out along the coast of California. Although today's southern sea otters are still endangered, their return has helped restore healthy kelp forests in Monterey Bay.

Everything Is Connected

Sea otters are one example of a **keystone species**, a species that's particularly important to its ecosystem. If you take a keystone species away, an ecosystem can crumble. On some level or another, every single species is important to its ecosystem—from a fist-sized limpet to a school bus–sized whale shark. This is an important concept in **ecology**, the study of organisms' interactions with each other and with their environments.

Marine animals form relationships with each other that help define their ecological roles. Two organisms might have a predator/prey relationship, like a sea otter and a sea urchin, or they might have a friendlier sort of relationship called **mutualism**. Mutualism occurs when two organisms of different species work together in a way that benefits both organisms, like when a cleaner wrasse cleans a moray eel's mouth by snacking on the stuff between the eel's teeth.

Some relationships aren't so mutual. The Greenland shark is the largest fish living in the Arctic Ocean, but even it has enemies. A small copepod called *Ommatokoita elongata* attaches to a Greenland shark's eyeballs, boring in and eating the eye tissue over a long period of time. The copepod benefits from the situation but damages the shark's eyes in the process. This is an example of **parasitism**, a relationship in which one organism benefits by harming the other.

In another type of ecological relationship called **commensalism**, one organism benefits and the other organism neither benefits nor is harmed. This can be a tough relationship to prove. One possible example is when barnacles attach to a whale's skin.

When a gray whale feeds on krill, any barnacles attached to the whale's head filter some of the plankton from the surrounding water. The

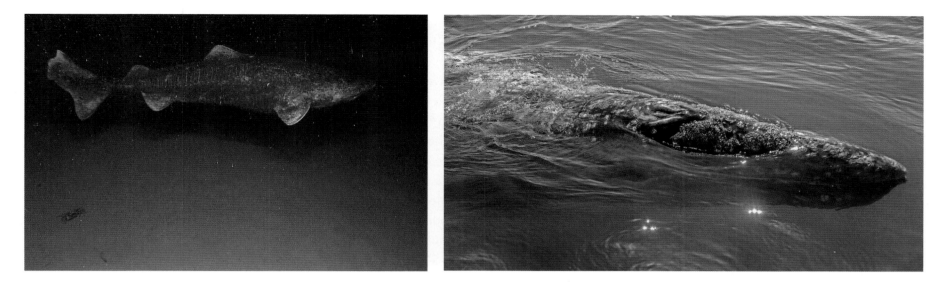

barnacles get a free meal, but does the whale mind that the barnacles are there? Most evidence suggests whales don't care whether the barnacles are there or not, but since scientists can't ask whales how they feel, it's difficult to say for sure. More research must be done.

Scientists may not fully understand all the relationships between organisms in an ecosystem, but it's clear that organisms depend on each other to survive. If you remove one single species from a community, the rest of the community will feel the loss in some way. Likewise, if you *add* one single species to a community, it forces the rest of the community to adapt. If an organism can't adapt to changes in its environment, it might find itself in big trouble.

The food chain is one of the best examples of how nature is connected. **Producers** start the food chain by using photosynthesis to create energy from the sun or by using chemosynthesis to create energy from chemicals like hydrogen sulfide. Algae and other phytoplankton are important producers in sunlit areas of lakes and the ocean.

Consumers eat producers and other consumers, passing energy up the food chain. In many cases, smaller fish get eaten by bigger fish, which get eaten by even bigger predators, such as marine mammals. At the top of the food chain are apex predators, consumers that aren't eaten by anything else in their natural environment. Examples of apex predators in marine food chains include orcas in the open ocean and polar bears in the Arctic.

Everything on Earth is linked—rivers, lakes, wetlands, oceans, and land. When humans create changes in the environment, they affect all of Earth's ecosystems on land and at sea. These changes force humans and the other animals that share the planet to adapt. It's time to start thinking about how our everyday actions impact our watery world.

(left) **A Greenland shark.**
NOAA OKEANOS Explorer Program, 2013 Northeast US Canyons Expedition

(right) **Barnacles are living on this gray whale's skin.**
Courtesy of Bruce Fryxell

Alien Invaders

When an alien species invades an ecosystem, it can be devastating for the animals that already live there. In ecology, alien species aren't from outer space; they're just from somewhere else on Earth. These aliens are also known as **invasive species**, disruptive organisms that are living in a place where they're not native.

In the ocean, lionfish living in the Atlantic Ocean are an invasive species. Lionfish are native to areas of the South Pacific and Indian Oceans. However, they are frequently caught and brought to new places so fish enthusiasts can keep them as pets in household aquariums. Sometimes, humans release their pets into the wild, not realizing that they are causing harm to the environment.

Since the 1980s, scientists have observed lionfish in the Atlantic Ocean along the southeastern coast of the United States. Humans who released lionfish into the ocean are the most likely cause. Because lionfish have few predators in this environment, they multiply quickly. As they do, they eat reef fish that are supposed to be living there, creating an imbalance in the ecosystem.

Lionfish in the Atlantic Ocean are an example of an invasive species.
Courtesy of Joel Warburton

Invasive species can also impact freshwater ecosystems, such as rivers and lakes. In the Great Lakes, zebra mussels have made their way from European waters to freshwater systems in North America with the help of cargo ships and the **ballast water** these ships transport from one place to another.

Here's how it works: After unloading cargo at a port, a cargo ship pumps water into special tanks to rebalance the ship for the return journey. This ballast water—and all the organisms living in it—get put back into the ocean when it's time to refill the ship with cargo at a different port. Sometimes, an alien species does well in its new environment, and that's when it becomes a problem.

Zebra mussels that hitched a ride in the ballast water of ships traveling from Europe to North America were quite successful in the Great Lakes. These plankton feeders have multiplied and spread to new freshwater ecosystems throughout North America, where they have reduced the amount of plankton available for native fish to eat.

Marine scientists study the impacts of invasive species and try to come up with plans to help marine and freshwater ecosystems get back to normal. Sometimes, this involves asking **citizen scientists** to report sightings of invasive species, such as zebra mussels in the Great Lakes. Since lionfish are edible and quite tasty, one strategy to reduce the number of invasive lionfish in the Atlantic is to encourage people to catch and eat them! Some restaurants have created gourmet lionfish dishes to help fuel demand.

MARINE SCIENCE PROFESSOR

Douglas McCauley, PhD

Marine Biologist
University of California Santa Barbara
Santa Barbara, California

"Being a marine scientist is oddly like being a painter, a rock star, or a politician. It often doesn't work out how you dreamed it would if you only put half your soul into it."

Doug McCauley grew up in Los Angeles, California, a place where the quickest way to access nature was to grab a mask and a snorkel and drive to the ocean, where some amazing animals live in the wild spaces just a stone's throw away from the bustle of California city life. Doug decided at six years old that he wanted to become a marine scientist. He remembers sitting by a tide pool and realizing that every species in the pool had its own amazing story.

Doug started working on fishing boats in middle school. He spent his time baiting hooks, dropping anchor, and scrubbing fish guts off the boat. The work was hard, but he loved being out on the ocean. In college, he started studying science. Just like in the tide pool, every marine animal he studied was like a piece of a puzzle—and each puzzle fit into an even bigger puzzle.

Today, Doug splits his time between teaching marine science to college students and conducting ocean research, studying sharks, tuna, parrotfish, giant sea bass, tropical seabirds, and other species. While conducting research, no day is the same. One day he and his team are putting satellite tags on the dorsal fins of sharks to see where they travel, another day they're taking tissue samples from manta rays to understand what they eat, and another day they spend hours swimming alongside endangered parrotfish to see how they affect the ecology of coral reefs.

As a marine scientist, Doug gets to follow his curiosities, help students discover what makes them curious, and use the power of science to help protect the ocean. Though it can be difficult to get a paid job as a marine scientist, he says if you're up for a challenge, it is one of the best jobs in the world.

Douglas McCauley, PhD.
Courtesy of Douglas McCauley

A Plastic Soup Ocean

In 1997, Charles Moore was sailing from Hawaii to California when he came across something that would change his life. It was a garbage patch in the middle of the Pacific Ocean. As Captain Moore stood on the deck of his research vessel, *Alguita*, and looked out across the sea, he saw trash floating in the water—including plastic bottle caps, plastic bags, and other debris that didn't belong there. This "trash island" is part of what is now known as the Great Pacific Garbage Patch.

Plastic is a human-made material that is designed to last. This can be a positive thing (when you drop a plastic ketchup bottle, it doesn't break), but it can also be a negative thing. Plastic doesn't break down as easily or naturally as other types of waste such as wood, grass, and food scraps.

When humans throw yogurt containers, shampoo bottles, and other packaging in the dumpster, all of this plastic ends up sitting in landfills, places where trash is buried in the Earth, for a long time.

Sometimes, trash doesn't even make it to trash-cans. When we toss fast-food wrappers out of car windows or leave empty plastic bottles on the ground, this litter could eventually end up floating in the ocean. When plastic ends up in the ocean, it slowly breaks down into smaller and smaller pieces, releasing chemicals into the water and creating what some people call "plastic soup."

A plastic soup ocean is bad for the animals that live there. Seabirds, fish, marine mammals, and marine reptiles such as sea turtles mistake small bits of plastic for food. When a seabird is foraging for food in the Great Pacific Garbage Patch, it might dive down and scoop up a piece of plastic,

Plastic pollution is dangerous for wildlife. *NOAA*

thinking it's something else. Scientists studying dead seabirds have found birds with stomachs full of plastic bottle caps and other plastic trash.

This is sad but not uncommon. Sea turtles are frequent victims of Earth's plastic problem. When a sea turtle sees a plastic bag floating in the ocean, it might eat the trash, thinking it's a tasty sea jelly.

Animals can't digest trash like they can digest food, so the plastic builds up in their systems. Many plastics also contain chemicals that can be dangerous if they end up inside an animal's stomach. Exposure to these chemicals can disrupt natural processes within animals' bodies.

Chemicals from factories, farms, and roads also end up in the ocean. Rain washes these chemicals from their sources into river systems. Then rivers act like drain pipes, eventually dumping the **pollution** into the sea. Even if your family lives far away from a coast and drives a car, the oil that drips from the car's engine onto the ground can end up polluting Earth's water supply.

When farmers use too much **fertilizer**, chemicals can leach into the water system and cause problems. Chemicals from fertilizers have the same effect in the water that they have on land—they cause plants to grow faster. In the ocean, these chemicals make phytoplankton, such as algae, grow out of control. When this happens, the algae use up a lot of oxygen and sometimes create a dead zone. Marine dead zones are areas that lack the oxygen most organisms need to survive.

Pesticides, which destroy pests, are other chemicals used in farming and growing. A par-

Toxic Algae

Phytoplankton plays an important role in the ocean. It is the base of most marine food chains, and all kinds of animals—from small sardines to massive blue whales—depend on it for survival. So it must be good for the ocean when there is a lot of phytoplankton floating around, right? It depends on how much and what type.

Too much phytoplankton can use up the oxygen in the water, killing the other organisms that live there or forcing them to move somewhere else. These **harmful algae blooms** can also cause trouble by blocking fishes' gills and suffocating underwater plants. Harmful algae blooms are sometimes called red tides because the blooms can make the water look red. However, experts prefer to use the term "harmful algae blooms" over "red tides," since the blooms can also appear brown, green, or colorless.

If the algae are toxic, the situation can become even worse. Some diatoms produce a toxin called domoic acid. As fish or shellfish eat diatoms and seabirds, other fish, and marine mammals eat the fish and shellfish, domoic acid can start making its way up the food chain. Sea lions are common victims of domoic acid poisoning. Once inside sea lions' bodies, the toxin changes their brains forever, disrupting the animals' short-term memories and making it harder for them to find food. In severe cases, domoic acid poisoning can cause death.

Harmful algae blooms affect humans too. When humans eat fish and shellfish that have toxins in their bodies, humans can suffer the same symptoms as other mammals affected by domoic acid poisoning. Toxic blooms may also affect the economy by forcing fisheries to close. In freshwater lakes and ponds, harmful algae blooms can contaminate drinking water.

ticularly harmful pesticide called DDT was used in the United States during and after World War II to keep insects from destroying important food crops. However, in the 1960s, environmentalists such as Rachel Carson, a biologist and author,

The Deepwater Horizon oil spill of 2010 polluted the ocean with millions of gallons of oil. *NOAA*

fought against the use of DDT after it was linked to unhealthy side effects in birds, fish, and humans that ate food contaminated by the chemical.

The United States banned the use of DDT in 1972, but other harmful chemicals continue to pollute Earth's waterways. Fertilizers and pesticides serve a purpose on land, so solving the problem is not as simple as telling people to stop using these chemicals. In everyday life, most of us contribute to the pollution of the ocean by using household cleaning products, bug sprays, and sunscreens filled with chemicals that can leach into the water system.

Costly Accidents

April 20, 2010, was an awful day for the planet. The Deepwater Horizon oil rig, a structure with equipment to drill into the seafloor and pull up oil

that humans need for energy and transportation, exploded in the middle of the Gulf of Mexico off the coast of Louisiana. The explosion caused millions of gallons of oil to spill into the ocean.

Whether caused by a freak accident, like the explosion of an oil rig, or a more typical accident, like the collision of two ships in the ocean, oil spills are unfortunately quite common. Oil and water don't mix; therefore, when oil spills into an ecosystem, the oil floats on the surface of the water and forms an oil slick.

Oil slicks are dangerous for wildlife. Immediately after the Deepwater Horizon oil spill of 2010, scientists began noticing how the oil was affecting the animals living in the Gulf of Mexico. Seabirds such as pelicans dove into the water to try to catch fish and then emerged with slick, oil-coated feathers.

Pelicans and other seabirds rely on their feathers to fly, float, and keep warm. Oily feathers make it more difficult for birds to do all three of these things. Since water doesn't clean oily feathers, oiled birds try to clean or preen their feathers with their beaks. When they do, they end up swallowing oil.

Brown pelicans and laughing gulls are two species of seabirds that particularly suffered after the Deepwater Horizon oil spill. The National Wildlife Federation estimates that 12 percent of the brown pelicans and 32 percent of the laughing gulls in the northern Gulf died because of the accident.

Other Gulf species such as Atlantic bluefin tuna, blue crabs, Kemp's ridley sea turtles, and deep-sea corals all suffered as a result of the 2010 oil spill. The spill also affected animals that ate food that had come in contact with the oil slick, including marine mammals such as bottlenose dolphins. Eating oil, like eating plastic, can cause an animal many health problems that lead to sickness or even death.

Cleaning up an oil spill in the ocean isn't easy. In the United States, organizations such as the Coast Guard and the Environmental Protection Agency are often responsible for containing an oil slick and trying to skim the oil from the surface of the water or using other cleanup methods without causing further harm to the environment. For example, the use of chemicals to disperse oil after a spill is a controversial cleanup method because these chemicals can also harm marine life.

Ship strikes, collisions between vessels and wildlife, are another type of accident that can harm an ecosystem. The ocean is like a highway for ships carrying goods between continents, and big ships sometimes run into animals in their paths. Whales are perhaps the most well-known victims of ship strikes. To help lower the risk, a ship traveling through certain areas must follow rules to lower its speed, use some lanes and not others, and keep a close watch for wildlife.

Fishing nets often end up capturing marine life that the fishermen didn't intend to catch. For instance, for every pound of shrimp a shrimp fishery catches, the fishery may also catch and throw away three or more pounds of unwanted species. This wasted catch, or **bycatch**, may include sharks and other fish, sea turtles, seabirds, and even marine mammals.

Bycatch is a problem because the animals that are caught accidentally are often killed in the process. To help reduce the number of sea turtles drowned as bycatch, NOAA scientists and shrimp fisheries in the United States have designed TEDs (turtle excluder devices). A TED is a grid of bars that can be fitted to the inside of a trawl net, a wide-mouthed net that's dragged along the bottom of the sea or pulled through the midwaters to trap fish. While small shrimp pass through the bars and stay in the trawl net, larger animals, such as turtles, can't pass through the bars. Instead, they escape through an opening in the net, hopefully unharmed.

Fishing nets that fisheries leave behind, on purpose or by accident, can also harm marine life.

Sea turtles can get trapped in fishing nets by accident.
Courtesy of Ülar Tikk

Clean Up an Oil Spill

What happens when oil spills into the ocean? Use common house-hold items to re-create an oil spill, observe how an oil slick interacts with water and wildlife, and then try to clean it up. This activity can get messy, so keep a trashcan and a dishcloth nearby to wipe your hands.

YOU'LL NEED

- Large clear bowl
- 4 cups of water
- Small container
- Food coloring (any color)
- 3 tablespoons of canola oil (if needed, substitute olive oil or another type of liquid cooking oil)
- Fake feather
- Cotton balls
- Sponge
- Spoon or soup ladle
- 2 squares of cheesecloth, 2 inches by 2 inches (5 cm by 5 cm)
- Dish soap

1. Fill a large clear bowl with 4 cups of water.

2. In a separate, small container, add 3–4 drops of food coloring to 3 tablespoons of canola oil. Stir the food coloring into the oil. The color and the oil will not mix very well, and that's OK.

3. Slowly pour the oil into the large bowl of water. Watch how the oil mixes (or doesn't mix) with the water.

4. Dip a fake feather halfway into the oil slick. When you pull the feather out, how does the wet part feel compared to the dry part?

5. Rinse the feather under running tap water. Does it rinse clean? Set the feather aside.

6. Next, try to remove some oil from the large bowl of water. Submerge most of a cotton ball in an oily spot on the water and let it soak. Once saturated, throw the cotton ball in the trash and repeat with a second cotton ball.

7. Dip a sponge into an oily spot on the water, let it soak for a few seconds, and then squeeze the oily water into your empty container. Try this twice.

8. See if you can scoop some more oil out of the bowl using a spoon or a soup ladle. Try to remove the oil without removing a lot of water with it. Empty the spoon or ladle into your separate container.

9. Dip a 2-by-2-inch (5-by-5-cm) square of cheesecloth into what's left of the oil slick and watch how it sops up oil. Repeat this step with a second square of cheesecloth.

10. Which cleanup method worked best for you? Use your favorite method to try to remove the rest of the oil from the bowl.

11. In a sink, use a few drops of dish soap to clean the oily feather you set aside earlier. Give it a good rinse, dry it with a towel, and fluff it up a bit. How does the feather feel now?

Extra Credit

In real life, oil cleanup methods include sorbent booms, skimmers, in situ burning, and dispersants. Take this activity up a notch by learning what these terms mean and seeing if you can design your own oil spill cleanup method.

Discarded "ghost nets" can float around for years, entangling crabs, sea turtles, seals and sea lions, and many other animals along the nets' deadly journeys. Animals that get trapped in ghost nets often drown because they can't escape on their own.

Humans' Bad Habits

For most people thinking about habitat loss, the first thing that comes to mind is the destruction of rain forests on land. It's true; humans are destroying rain forests for resources such as wood for furniture, construction materials, and paper products. Humans are also destroying wetlands to make way for houses, buildings, and parking lots. In some cases, wetlands are being drained and the water redirected to support nearby towns and agricultural fields. For the species that rely on wetland ecosystems, this can be disastrous.

Human development also affects rivers and lakes. Human-made dams, large concrete structures that hold river water back, can negatively impact an ecosystem by changing how rivers flow. These barriers decrease the amount of water on one side of the dam and increase the amount of water on the other side, which can destroy the plants that used to make up the riverbank.

Dams also block the way for migrating animals. If a sockeye salmon is traveling upstream to spawn and it reaches a dam, it can't finish its journey without some help. By building fish ladders into dams, humans provide some help. A fish ladder is a series of small pools, each one higher than the next, like a staircase. To climb a fish ladder, fish leap from pool to pool, gaining elevation with each leap and taking rests when they're tired. Once the fish climb the fish ladder, they can continue their migration.

There are positive effects of dams alongside the negative ones. Some dams provide humans with drinking water and/or water to irrigate nearby farmlands. Other dams help prevent floods by collecting rainwater and then releasing the extra water slowly back into the river. Dams can also be used to produce **hydropower** by turning flowing water into electricity.

The decision to build a new dam must be taken seriously because of the impact it could have on the river ecosystem. In recent years, some people have fought to remove dams that have already been built. A large dam removal project in Washington State called the Elwha River Restoration began in 2011 and lasted until 2014. The US National Park Service demolished the Elwha Dam and the Glines Canyon Dam in an effort to help rebuild the Elwha River ecosystem.

Habitat destruction is also a problem out in the middle of the ocean, far away from where humans live. A method of fishing called dredging involves dragging a large metal-framed basket along the seafloor. Fisheries use dredges to catch shellfish such as clams and oysters living on the bottom of the ocean. Dredges and bottom trawl nets disturb fragile seafloor ecosystems.

Irresponsible fishing methods can also destroy coral reef habitats. In some cases, humans use poison or even dynamite to stun reef fish so they're easier to collect. These methods can destroy the surrounding coral reef. Since coral takes so long to grow, and because coral reefs are home to so many species, this is a tragic loss.

Overhunting is another way humans are damaging the ocean ecosystem. Whaling, the killing of whales for their meat, blubber, or other resources, is a form of hunting in the ocean that was common in past centuries. In some communities, whale meat, whale oil, and baleen were important to humans' way of life. But humans began killing too many whales, and several whale species became endangered.

Multiple whaling nations came together and agreed to stop most forms of whaling, forming the International Whaling Commission (IWC) in 1946. Thanks to the IWC's efforts, many whale populations are slowly recovering. However, it's difficult to enforce rules in international waters. Whaling still exists today in some countries, such as Iceland and Japan.

Fish and shellfish are an extremely important food source for millions of people, but too much fishing can have the same effect on fish as whaling had on whales. Overfishing is bad not only for the animals being hunted but also for humans. As the overfished species' numbers decline, there are fewer and fewer of them to catch. Eventually, the people relying on these fish must rely on something else. With some care and caution, the global community can work together to find a balance between fishing and overfishing.

Sometimes, fish are overfished or illegally fished for just one part of their bodies. Shark fin soup is a traditional dish served in China. The global demand for this soup, particularly in Asia, has led to shark finning, a practice in which a fisherman briefly catches a shark, slices off its fins, and then releases it back into the water. Even if it's still alive when released, the finless shark will soon die. Shark finning has led to a declining number of sharks in the world's oceans.

Manta rays are similarly threatened, thanks to a demand for their feathery gill rakers, or gill plates. Manta rays rely on their gill plates to filter plankton from the water. In traditional Chinese medicine, dried manta gill plates are said to cure all kinds of diseases, but there is no medical evidence that this is true.

A Big Change

By heating and cooling homes and buildings and by filling planes, trains, and automobiles with gasoline, scientists believe humans are creating a big change in the environment. Many everyday human activities, such as driving a car, release gases like carbon dioxide into the air. These gases build up in the atmosphere over time, trapping heat from the sun and causing the Earth's temperature to rise. Scientists call this **global warming**.

Global warming causes the ocean's temperature to get warmer too. Marine scientists are concerned about warming ocean temperatures for a few reasons. One reason is rising sea levels. Warm water takes up more space than cold water, so as the ocean's temperature rises, the ocean expands. For people who live on low-lying islands, this is a scary thought. If sea levels rise just 16 feet (5 m),

Manta rays are under threat because they are being hunted for their gill plates. *NOAA*

a small island in the Pacific Ocean called Tuvalu could disappear completely under the sea.

Adding to the problem of rising sea levels is another effect of global warming: melting ice. As temperatures rise near the North and South Poles, ice sheets that cover landmasses such as Greenland and Antarctica are melting and adding to the total volume of water in the oceans. More water equals higher sea levels.

Glaciers are also melting in the Arctic Ocean, creating problems for Arctic wildlife. The most famous example of how global warming is harming wildlife involves the iconic polar bear. Polar bears are the apex predators of the Arctic food chain, but each year, as the sea ice shrinks, it hurts these creatures' ability to hunt.

Polar bears rely on the sea ice to catch ringed seals and other marine mammals—their main source of food. Ringed seals also depend on sea ice to raise their pups. In fact, many animals living above the ice and below it rely on the sea ice to survive, including belugas and narwhals—whales that have long twisted tusks sticking out of their heads. If the ocean continues to warm, the animals living in the Arctic and Antarctic regions face uncertain futures.

Coral reefs also suffer when ocean temperatures rise. When conditions in the ocean change, such as when the water temperature becomes colder or warmer, the helpful algae living inside coral polyps may become stressed and leave. Without the colorful algae, the coral looks white. This phenomenon, called **coral bleaching**, weakens the coral because it can no longer rely on the algae for energy and nutrients. Coral can sometimes recover from coral-bleaching events, but often they don't.

Ocean acidification is another change that can harm coral reefs. The ocean absorbs a lot of the carbon dioxide that humans are adding to the atmosphere. Over time, this makes the ocean more acidic. More acid in the ocean makes it less friendly to organisms that, like corals, have calcium carbonate skeletons, which can weaken and eventually start to dissolve in acidic environments.

Earth's marine and freshwater ecosystems are in trouble. Because everything is connected, even small changes in an environment can start a chain reaction that could end up causing a species' extinction.

Much damage has been done, and it's important for marine scientists to understand this, but it is also important to remain hopeful. The ocean may be changing, but it is still a remarkably wild place filled with wonders. Just think—the biggest animal that ever lived is still out there swimming just a few miles from the shore!

In the next chapter, you'll read about some of the ways people are helping to turn things around for the ocean and Earth's freshwater ecosystems. Governments, scientists and researchers, and ordinary citizens must all work together to make sure animals like sea otters, blue whales, and polar bears don't go extinct on our watch.

Polar bears are important Arctic predators that rely on sea ice.
Courtesy of KT Miller/ Polarbearsinternational.org

Experiment with Ocean Acidification

The ocean is becoming more acidic. What impact will this have on marine organisms with skeletons or shells made out of calcium carbonate? Conduct an experiment to compare what happens to an eggshell that sits in tap water for 24 hours with what happens to an eggshell that sits in vinegar, an acidic liquid, for 24 hours.

*Before you begin, form a **hypothesis**, an educated guess about the outcome. What will happen to the eggshell that soaks in vinegar for a full day?*

YOU'LL NEED

- 2 bowls
- 1 cup of water
- 1 cup of white vinegar
- Pen or pencil
- Paper
- 1 egg

Water   Vinegar

1. Label the two bowls using two small strips of paper, one that says WATER and one that says VINEGAR. Add 1 cup of water to the bowl labeled WATER and 1 cup of white vinegar to the bowl labeled VINEGAR.

2. Carefully crack an egg against the side of a sink or the edge of a bowl and empty the shell, keeping as much of the eggshell intact as possible. (You can throw away the rest of the egg or save it in a small container to use for food later.)

3. Choose two pieces of eggshell that are about the same size. Pieces that are about 1 inch (2½ cm) long by 1 inch (2½ cm) wide work well.

4. Place one of the eggshell pieces in the bowl of water and place the second eggshell piece in the bowl of vinegar. Each eggshell piece should be completely submerged. Take note of the time.

5. Come back after a few hours and take a look at the eggshells in the bowls. Has there been any change? What observations can you make?

6. Leave the eggshells in their bowls until 24 hours has passed from the start of the experiment.

7. After 24 hours, carefully remove the eggshells from the bowls. How would you describe the eggshell that has been in vinegar compared to the eggshell that has been in tap water? Does this result support your hypothesis?

Extra Credit

Write a science report about ocean acidification. In the report, define *ocean acidification* and discuss what it could mean for coral reefs and other marine organisms.

Play Ecosystem Jenga

In an ecosystem, everything is connected. When there's a change, such as a species' extinction, it affects the entire ecosystem, often making it less stable. Play a marine science version of Jenga to explore this idea. The game can be played solo or with as many friends as you'd like.

YOU'LL NEED

- Jenga, or a similar tower game
- Dice (as many as your group would like, based on the number of players)

Objective

Keep your ecosystem (the block tower) from toppling over for as long as possible. Make the connection between how removing blocks from the tower is similar to the way environmental problems make an ecosystem less stable over time.

Setup

Follow the set of instructions included with the Jenga set to stack the wooden blocks. If you're playing with a group, determine who goes first, second, third, and so on. Read the "How to Play" and "Additional Rules" sections before you start the game.

How to Play

The first player begins the game by rolling one of the dice. Next, read the description from the list below that matches the number you rolled, and take whatever action it calls for. If you're playing with a group, read the description and the action out loud.

1. A fishing boat drags a bottom trawl net through your ecosystem. Remove one block.
2. Two cargo ships collide several miles away, spilling oil into the ocean that will eventually reach your ecosystem. Remove two blocks.
3. A group of volunteers picks up trash that could have entangled wildlife in your ecosystem. Add one block.
4. A species in your ecosystem becomes extinct. Remove three blocks.
5. A law passes that creates a protected area near your ecosystem. Add one block.
6. The water in your ecosystem is becoming warmer and more acidic as the global climate slowly changes. Remove one block.

Additional Rules

When the action includes *removing* a block, follow the Jenga rules for doing so. These include using *one hand* to carefully remove the block from any row except the top, adding the block to the top of the tower, and then waiting 10 seconds before the next player takes a turn. Players can take their time choosing which blocks are loose enough to remove by giving them a gentle poke.

When the action description includes *adding* a block, remove the last block added to the tower and fill in a space where the block will make the stack more stable. Other players can give you advice if you want it. Players can use both hands to keep the stack stable as they add blocks.

In the first round, if the first player rolls a three or a five, have the player roll again until he or she rolls something other than a three or a five.

The game ends when the tower falls. In real life, ecosystems aren't always doomed to crumble like a tower of Jenga blocks, but they can if the ecosystems don't have enough time to adapt to negative changes. Sometimes, humans can step in and make positive changes that help an ecosystem recover.

Extra Credit

Create your own version of Ecosystem Jenga by selecting a marine ecosystem, coming up with six potential changes (some positive and some negative), and then choosing what actions players should take for each change.

7

Making a Difference

Suspended in the tropical waters of the Indian Ocean off the coast of the Maldives, Andrea Marshall is surrounded by hundreds of manta rays. The mantas barrel through the water, mouths agape, feeding on swarms of plankton. Marshall is used to being a small diver in a sea of large mantas, but as the fish swarm around her, she feels her heart beat a little faster. She'll remember this moment as one of her most exciting dives ever.

Marshall has been in love with the sea her whole life. Starting when she was about five years old, Marshall told anyone who would listen that she wanted to be a marine biologist, a person who studies marine life. Her particular wish was to study sharks and rays.

As the director of the manta ray program for the Marine Megafauna Foundation, a **conservation** organization Marshall cofounded with her friend Simon Pierce, she has made her dream come true. Marshall travels the globe and spends hours in the water swimming alongside some of the most magnificent animals in the world.

Andrea Marshall, PhD, swims alongside a manta ray.
Courtesy of Andrea Marshall

Marshall's favorite moments come when she is diving one-on-one with a single manta. She says, "To be midwater with an enormous animal, like a giant [manta], and have them 'play' with you is an extraordinary sensation. I also like the feeling I get when a manta actively looks for an encounter with me. They will approach you underwater from out of nowhere, interact with you for a while, and then without warning decide that they are finished. Sometimes, I feel as if I am the one being examined!"

While her life as a marine scientist can be exciting, it's also a lot of work. Marshall works long hours, sometimes seven days a week, in some of the harshest and most remote areas of the world. She goes without many luxuries in life and, like other scientists and researchers, she and her team spend a lot of time in front of computers writing reports.

Marshall got where she is today thanks to many years of dedication. In fact, she earned a PhD before she was 30 years old. She has contributed a lot to the scientific community's understanding of manta ray's biology, ecology, and behavior, and she continues to build a legacy by educating the next generation of marine scientists.

It's easy to get caught up in all the problems facing the ocean, but Marshall says, "Nothing keeps you going like seeing a problem and wanting to help solve it." In this final chapter, you will learn how many people, including governments, conservation organizations, and individuals are working together to solve big problems in creative ways.

Setting Boundaries

Many nations across the globe are helping to protect marine and freshwater ecosystems from harm by setting some boundaries or rules. Rules can help reduce the negative impacts humans have on natural places by managing the way we interact with these places.

Marine protected areas (MPAs) are aquatic areas that are protected for conservation purposes by law. MPAs can include intertidal zones, near-shore habitats such as kelp forests and coral reefs, large areas of the open ocean, deep-sea habitats, freshwater ecosystems, and wetlands.

A government may create an MPA to preserve an ecosystem's **biodiversity**, the variety of life in that ecosystem; to provide a safe place for fish species to reproduce and recover from overfishing; to protect an endangered species; or to prevent an area from being damaged by human activities—or all of the above. One important MPA encompasses the largest living structure in the world—the Great Barrier Reef. The Australian government created the Great Barrier Reef Marine Park as part of the Great Barrier Reef Marine Park Act of 1975.

In the United States, there are different kinds of MPAs depending on an area's needs. In some cases, the rules prevent humans from building structures on a protected coastline. In other cases, the rules restrict how much shellfish a fishery can catch within an MPA. In all cases, the rules are there to protect natural resources such as fish and shellfish or to preserve cultural resources such as a shipwreck.

In 2016, the United States government expanded an MPA called the Papahānaumokuākea Marine National Monument to encompass about 583,000 square miles (1.5 million km²) of land and sea surrounding the northwestern Hawaiian Islands. Papahānaumokuākea is home to thousands of marine species, including the endangered Hawaiian monk seal.

Also in 2016, the British government announced it would create a marine reserve around Ascension Island in the Atlantic Ocean. The island, together with its surrounding waters, is an important habitat for endangered species such as the green turtle and vulnerable species such as the Ascension frigatebird.

Governments can also help protect marine environments by passing laws that restrict destructive practices on land. Laws may regulate the use of harmful chemicals, such as the US government's ban on DDT, or they may set goals for cleaner air and cleaner water.

In 2015, a bill banning the sale of soaps, toothpastes, and other rinse-off products that contain **plastic microbeads** became a law in the United States. When these tiny plastic beads go down the drain, they end up in rivers, lakes, and the ocean. Once there, microbeads absorb pollutants from the surrounding water. Fish and other marine animals eat the microbeads, thinking they're food. Toxins build up in animals' bodies as they're passed from one organism to the next as part of the food chain. Eventually, the toxins may end up in the seafood on someone's dinner plate.

In some US states, laws restrict the use of plastic grocery bags or single-use packaging products such as Styrofoam containers. While the ocean's trash problem is vast, rules that limit the use of materials that could end up in the ocean can help keep the problem from getting worse.

Laws may also protect threatened or endangered species from being hunted or fished. The Marine Mammal Protection Act, enacted in the United States in 1972, is one example. The law prevents people from hunting or harming marine mammals in and around US waters.

In 2016, the US government expanded the Papahānaumokuākea Marine National Monument significantly, bringing the total protected area to 582,578 square miles (over 1.5 million km²). *NOAA*

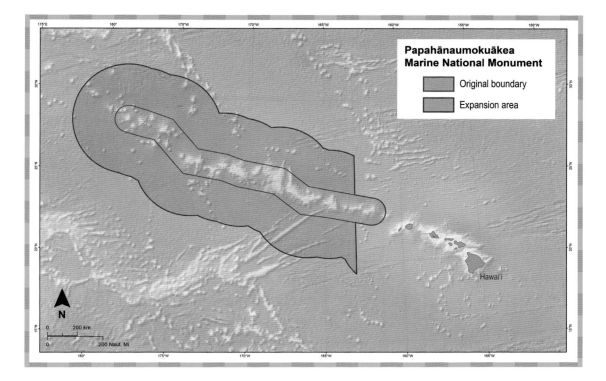

It is illegal to hunt or harm marine mammals, like humpback whales, in many parts of the world. *NOAA*

part of the marine science community because they work toward providing this information.

Research and Conservation

Randy Wells has been studying dolphins for the past 45 years. As a senior conservation scientist for the Chicago Zoological Society and director of the Sarasota Dolphin Research Program based in Sarasota, Florida, Wells knows just how important research is in protecting marine mammals and other marine creatures. His research has spanned many marine mammal species, including several species of whales and dolphins, as well as vaquitas and manatees. He now leads teams that perform research to learn more about dolphins' health, their methods of communication, and their responses to human interactions.

The problems facing Earth are global, and, therefore, the solutions must be global too. Leaders and scientists from all around the world come together periodically to talk about the challenges facing the planet, including those that impact the ocean, such as global warming and ocean acidification, and then come up with plans to address these challenges. The United Nations Environment Programme is one example of an international group that leads global efforts to address environmental issues affecting the planet.

Before governments can pass laws to protect marine and freshwater ecosystems, scientists must first know how these ecosystems work and how humans are making an impact in these places. Research and conservation groups are a critical

Marine scientists at the Sarasota Dolphin Research Program study dolphins in their natural environment and make discoveries about how the dolphins live their lives in the face of many environmental challenges. From their findings, the scientists provide key information that can lead to better dolphin conservation efforts.

The people who are part of the research program also have a direct impact on the lives of the dolphins in Sarasota Bay. Wells recalls a memorable encounter with a Sarasota Bay resident—a young dolphin the researchers named Scrappy. In July 2006, researchers observed over a period of two weeks that Scrappy had some kind of material draped over his back and around his body. It was clearly not going to come off without some help.

Randy Wells, PhD. *Courtesy of Randy Wells*

Marine scientists as part of the Sarasota Dolphin Research Program observe dolphins in their natural environment. *Courtesy of Randy Wells (photo taken under National Marine Fisheries Service Scientific Research Permit)*

The Sarasota Dolphin Research Program received permission from the government to attempt a rescue. Wells and his team caught up with Scrappy and brought him aboard a specially designed boat. Once Scrappy was on board, the team discovered he was entangled in a pair of men's swim trunks that had cut deeply into his flippers.

Veterinarians removed the material, gave Scrappy some medicine to help him fight off infection, and released the dolphin back into the bay. Wells says the research team has seen Scrappy hundreds of times since then, and he appears to be in good condition.

Research and conservation go hand-in-hand, because without data, it's impossible for scientists to know whether an ecosystem is healthy or unhealthy. Similarly, if scientists don't know how healthy dolphins act, how will they know when the dolphins are unhealthy? If scientists don't know how many rays usually live in an area, how will they know if the rays are being overfished?

Organizations like the Marine Megafauna Foundation rely on scientific research to develop recommendations and proposals for local governments and international conservation groups that can help protect species and habitats. Andrea Marshall's research on manta rays helped get these animals listed with the Convention on International Trade in Endangered Species of Wild Fauna and Flora (CITES), an international agreement among nations that helps prevent international trade from threatening a species' survival.

Project Seahorse is another organization that focuses on conducting research and turning its

SOCIAL SCIENTIST

Peter Edwards, PhD

Economist and Social Science Coordinator
NOAA Coral Reef Conservation Program
Silver Spring, Maryland

"Planet Earth is all we have; nurture her."

Born and raised in Jamaica, a tropical island in the Caribbean, Peter Edwards spent many of his childhood summers at the beach and with his grandparents in rural inland areas of the island. Living on a tropical island made Peter feel connected to the ocean, and he decided to pursue a career in ecology, with a focus on marine biology.

Peter wants to help people and governments understand the true value of natural resources such as coral reefs. His current job as a marine scientist includes leading a team that studies the humans living near coral reefs in places like Florida, American Samoa, Guam, the US Virgin Islands, Puerto Rico, and Hawaii.

He asks people what they know about reefs and how they interact with them. Their responses help scientists come up with new strategies to protect coral reefs and all the organisms that live there—from algae and sea grass to reef fish, lobsters, and sharks.

Peter's average day includes coordinating calls and meetings and working with all sorts of scientists to come up with solutions to tough conservation issues affecting coral reefs. From time to time, he also gets to travel to places that have corals—from Mexico to tiny islands such as Kosrae and Yap.

When people understand that nearby reefs are valuable to their communities, Peter says they're more likely to take care of those reefs. When Peter gets the chance to talk to kids about becoming marine scientists, he likes to say, "Be curious about the world and everything in it! This will require paying attention to math and science in school, not only biology but chemistry and physics as well. You never know where you'll end up. But most important, follow your passion!"

Peter Edwards, PhD.
Courtesy of K. Desai

findings into conservation action, in this case to benefit seahorses, their relatives, and their marine ecosystems. One way Project Seahorse conducts research is by asking ordinary people to become citizen scientists.

iSeahorse is Project Seahorse's citizen science program, which involves people all around the world in supporting seahorse conservation and science. The iSeahorse website and smartphone app allow citizen scientists to share their wild seahorse

Conduct Wildlife Research

Science doesn't have to happen in a special lab. Citizen scientists conduct research to help the scientific community collect data. You can practice wildlife research using the same technique scientists and citizen scientists use: observation. This activity requires access to an animal you can observe for at least 15 minutes.

YOU'LL NEED

- Notebook
- Pen or pencil
- Timer or stopwatch
- Binoculars (optional)
- Magnifying glass (optional)

Preparation

Plan with an adult how you'd like to complete this activity. You can observe a pet at home; you can observe wildlife in a backyard or a nearby park; you can spend the afternoon in nature, such as at a beach with tide pools or at a national park; or you can visit a zoo or aquarium.

If you choose to visit a zoo or aquarium, select one that's accredited by the Association of Zoos and Aquariums and/or the World Association of Zoos and Aquariums. Accredited zoos and aquariums meet high standards for animal care and participate in important conservation, research, and education programs.

Observation

Set up your observation station with a notebook and a pen or pencil, a timer or stopwatch, and any other tools you may need, such as a pair of binoculars for observing an animal from far away or a magnifying glass for observing an animal up close.

Set a timer for 15 minutes. During the next 15 minutes, try not to change the animal's behavior by disturbing it in any way.

As you observe the animal, take notes in your notebook. What does the animal look like? Make a quick sketch.

What is the animal doing? Every time the animal does something new during the 15-minute period, write it down.

After 15 minutes is up, extend the activity by choosing another animal, observing it for 15 minutes, and then comparing your two sets of notes.

Extra Credit

If you could observe any marine animal in the wild, what would it be? White sharks? Polar bears? Sea otters? Deep-sea siphonophores? Pretend you are a marine scientist doing research work in the field. Use what you know about the animal to write imaginary observations on a new notebook page (or look it up online to learn more). Sketch the animal as if you could really see it.

sightings and observations. All of this data taken together contributes to the scientific community's knowledge of seahorses and, ultimately, their conservation.

Some organizations help rally public support for conservation projects and raise awareness about conservation issues. Mission Blue is one such organization led by Sylvia Earle, who famously said, "People ask 'Why should I care about the ocean?' It seems so obvious . . . it's the blue heart of the planet. We should take care of our heart; it's what makes life possible for us."

Mission Blue educates people about Hope Spots, areas of the ocean that need protection, and works to increase the number of protected places in the ocean. The organization even created a documentary called *Mission Blue* (2014) that helps spread the organization's message through film.

Creative Problem Solving

While diving off the coast of Greece, a young Dutch inventor named Boyan Slat made a disturbing discovery. He and his friend saw more plastic bags in this underwater environment than fish. Slat was particularly troubled. Tiny bits of plastic littered the ocean and the beaches where he was spending his vacation. Worse, he knew the problem extended far beyond what he could see. He wondered, *Why can't we just clean up the ocean?* When Slat returned home, he started working on a solution to the ocean's plastic problem as part of a school project.

What began as a school project became something much more. Slat started asking questions and conducting scientific experiments to find answers. For instance, he wanted to know if there was a way to filter plastic out of the water without also removing plankton.

In February 2013, as an 18-year-old, Slat founded a nonprofit organization called the Ocean Cleanup. He and the Ocean Cleanup team began designing a large-scale system of floating barriers

The ocean is the blue heart of Planet Earth.
Courtesy of Bruce Fryxell

attached to the seabed. As seawater flows past the barriers, the system separates plastics from the water and funnels them to a collection point. Scientists are still studying whether the system will work, but the Ocean Cleanup's goal is to use its system to start cleaning up the Great Pacific Garbage Patch by 2020.

Many other people have come up with creative solutions that can help tackle some of the issues facing the ocean. Ken Nedimyer and the Coral Restoration Foundation developed the Coral Tree Nursery to help rebuild coral reef ecosystems in the Florida Keys. Since 2010, Nedimyer's team has been building simple treelike PVC pipe structures that attach to the seabed. The team hangs fragments of coral, such as staghorn coral and elkhorn coral, from the branches of the "tree" as it floats in the ocean water column.

For about six to nine months, the coral fragments grow in the Coral Tree Nursery. Once the fragments grow big enough, volunteers and staff at the Coral Restoration Foundation remove the corals from the nursery and attach them to local reefs using glue that works underwater. The idea is that the coral transplants will continue to grow in the wild, bringing new life to reefs that have, in some cases, begun to die.

As coral reefs around the world suffer from the effects of ocean acidification and global warming, replenishing reefs with nursery-grown corals could be an important strategy in saving the ocean's coral habitats. Scientists are still researching the long-term success of such efforts and continue to look for ways to make the process easier and faster.

A "tree" made of PVC pipe acts as a nursery for staghorn corals. *NOAA*

Technology will be an important tool for the next generation of marine scientists as they come up with new ideas to address the problems facing marine and freshwater ecosystems. From satellite tags that track an endangered species' migration patterns to scientific and engineering breakthroughs that allow humans to create and use more sustainable (eco-friendly) materials for building and packaging, there is plenty of hope in the fight to save Planet Earth.

The most important step each person can take for the planet is to think about how his or her own actions are affecting the natural world. Humans can't rely on cleanup solutions and technology

You'll find suggestions for simple, positive changes you and your family can make at the end of this chapter.

to do all of the hard work; we must change our behavior so we stop adding to the problem.

Working in Marine Science

Marine scientists are the warriors battling for a healthy Earth. Whether they're researching rockfish ecology, taking care of injured wildlife, writing articles about global warming, or educating the public about marine life at a zoo or aquarium, each marine scientist can make a difference in his or her own way.

Josh, coauthor, poses with Harpo, a male California sea lion. *Authors' collection*

Let's take a closer look at what it's like to work as a real-life marine scientist. When Andrea Marshall of the Marine Megafauna Foundation is in the field (working outside of an office or lab), she and her team wake up early in the morning and get out on the water as soon as they can. Marshall usually dives two to five times with manta rays, making observations and collecting data on the mantas and their surrounding habitat. She then spends the afternoon prepping gear for the next day and doing data entry.

When Marshall and her team are not in the field, they spend their time on computers, inputting and processing the data they collected in the field. They must write papers and try to publish their results in scientific journals so the information can be available to the rest of the marine science community.

At the Sarasota Dolphin Research Program, the scientists' days are also a mixed bag of field days and office days. Randy Wells says a typical field day in his program involves heading out on a small boat with a small team of researchers for about eight hours, searching for dolphin groups and observing each group, collecting environmental and behavioral data, and photographing the dorsal fin of each dolphin. The dorsal fin photos are like ID cards that researchers can use to identify the dolphins later.

For each fun day in the field, there are usually one or two days in the lab for processing and analyzing data. As the program director, Wells spends most days in the office, seeking funds for the

AQUARIUM EDUCATOR

Emily Yam

Science Interpretation Supervisor
Aquarium of the Pacific
Long Beach, California

"When I tell some people that I work at an aquarium, they ask me if I take care of animals. I always tell them that I work with two-legged animals—humans!"

Emily Yam didn't grow up by the ocean, but she was a fan of slimy creatures, particularly salamanders and frogs. While Emily was in college studying biology and education, she had a summer job at the National Science Foundation, a government office that provides money for scientific research.

One day she heard a speaker talk about some research being done in Antarctica. Amazed by the pictures and stories, Emily asked the speaker how she could get involved. Eight months later, she was on an icebreaking research vessel studying krill in the Southern Ocean. That's when she fell in love with the sea.

Emily spent several more years working in the field and in a lab. She got to dive in submarines and explore ancient mountains far below the surface, studying the rocks and animals found there. She went to college again to earn a graduate degree. While there, she studied plankton, the tiny ocean drifters that are so important to marine food chains.

After graduate school, Emily found a job that combined her love of marine science and education. She moved to California and started working at the Aquarium of the Pacific, where she teaches kids, oversees staff, and works on special projects. Her most important responsibility is to think of ways to make science interesting for everyone who comes through the door of the aquarium.

Emily says the most difficult part of her job is also the best part of her job—she must be creative in connecting with people and then helping them connect to the ocean. Just like there are lots of ways to be a scientist, there are also lots of ways to be a teacher. Emily is both a scientist and a teacher, and her classroom is an aquarium dedicated to educating the public.

Emily Yam.
Courtesy of the
Aquarium of the Pacific

Working with Marine Mammals

Do you like waking up before the sun rises? Does the thought of cleaning up after animals make you happy? How about living out of a tent and not showering for weeks at a time? If you answered yes to any of these questions, working with marine mammals may be your calling.

One way to work with marine mammals is to become an animal care specialist or keeper at a zoo or aquarium. A typical day as a marine-mammal keeper includes preparing food (often by cutting up fish), feeding the animals, and cleaning their exhibits. A marine-mammal keeper's day also usually includes several training sessions.

A keeper's most important training goal is to teach an animal how to participate in its own health care. For instance, if Troy the harbor seal learns how to lie on a scale without being scared, it makes weighing him much easier for the staff members who want to make sure he's healthy.

Keepers constantly work to make sure the animals in their care are happy and healthy. Though it is hard work, the rewards are great. Marine-mammal keepers get to build trusting relationships with animals that often have a lot of personality. Educating the public is a big part of a keeper's job too. When keepers educate zoo and aquarium guests about marine mammals, they're inspiring people to care about the ocean and all the creatures in it.

Working at rescue and rehabilitation centers is another option for those who want to take care of marine mammals. The Marine Mammal Care Center (MMCC) in San Pedro, California, is one example of a center that helps sick, injured, or stranded pinnipeds get healthy, before releasing them back into the ocean.

Volunteers and a handful of paid staff members run the MMCC in shifts. During certain times of the year, the workday lasts from 4 AM to 6 PM. Duties include prepping formula for young seals and sea lions, hand-feeding them, and cleaning up after them. It's hard work, but it's a great way to make a difference in the lives of marine mammals.

Becoming a veterinarian that specializes in marine mammals is another rewarding career choice. Veterinarians working at zoos and aquariums play an important role in maintaining marine mammals' health. Vets in charge of rescue and rehabilitation centers focus on helping the animals get healthy as quickly as possible so they can be released safely.

Wildlife researchers studying marine mammals get to observe these animals in their natural habitats. Some researchers study whale behavior by watching whales from a boat. Other researchers study sea lion behavior by camping out in a remote place and monitoring a sea lion colony for weeks at a time. From keeper work to field research, if you have a passion for marine mammals, there are many ways to make your dream come true.

research, managing staff and budgets, networking with other marine scientists, and preparing scientific papers.

There is no set job description for a marine scientist because there are so many different types—from oceanographers and marine biologists to aquarists and keepers, conservationists, wildlife researchers, and environmental engineers. People with all kinds of backgrounds and skills can contribute to the marine science community. These people include teachers and other educators, writers and journalists, and photographers and other visual storytellers, such as filmmakers.

Start Today

Here are some tips for getting started in your career as a marine scientist. First, think about what gets you excited. Are you like Asha de Vos, who gets excited about whale poo and its importance for marine ecosystems? Are you passionate about protecting sharks from shark finning? Next, think about your skill set. What are you good at doing? What are your favorite subjects in school? No matter how you answered these questions, there is a way for you to use your skills to make a difference.

Most careers in marine science require a strong science background. Pay close attention in science classes, ask a parent or guardian to take you to museums of natural history and science, and try to spend time outside learning more about the world around you. Watch educational TV instead of regular TV and remember to always be curious.

Ask questions and try to find answers. Read more books like *Marine Science for Kids* and create your own marine science–based activities to do at home.

When you reach college age, consider choosing a major in science. Volunteer at a local aquarium to help educate guests. Participate in citizen science projects to gain experience. Organize your own observation and research projects for practice. Above all, learn about the issues facing Earth's marine and freshwater ecosystems and look for ways to create positive change.

There's no reason to wait until you're grown-up to start making a difference for the animals you care about and the natural places you enjoy. Even if you don't plan to become a marine scientist,

Stranded sea lion pups have the chance to recover at the MMCC before being released back into the wild. *Courtesy of Katrina Plummer / The Marine Mammal Care Center, San Pedro, California*

All photographs were taken during stranding response activities conducted under a Stranding Agreement between National Marine Fisheries Service and Marine Mammal Care Center at Fort MacArthur issued under the authority of the Marine Mammal Protection Act.

Interview a Marine Scientist

The best way to learn what it's really like to be a marine scientist is to ask one. Pretend you're a reporter as you interview a professional working in this field.

YOU'LL NEED

- Pen or pencil
- Notebook

1. Brainstorm with an adult about how you can get in touch with a marine scientist. Many scientists at universities and research or conservation organizations share their e-mail addresses online. Use the "Resources" page at the back of this book as a starting point to find some marine science organizations.

2. Think about what you'd like to know, and then write down some questions. You could include questions such as "Why did you become a marine scientist?" and "How can I make a difference for marine life?"

3. Ask an adult to help you coordinate the interview. Depending on the situation, it might be best to conduct the interview in person, on the phone, or via e-mail. Be sure to take notes if you conduct the interview in person or on the phone.

4. After the interview, sit down with a parent, guardian, or teacher and come up with a plan to participate in the marine science community. For instance, do you want to start using less plastic? Do you want to organize a trash cleanup day in your neighborhood?

5. Write your marine scientist a thank-you note for his or her time. Include a few sentences in the note that talks about your plan.

Tip

If you can't get in touch with a marine scientist, try this instead. Sit down and brainstorm what you've learned by reading *Marine Science for Kids*. Which chapter was your favorite? Which marine scientist did you like reading about? Next, come up with a plan to begin your own journey as a marine scientist.

Earth is everyone's home, and it's up to each and every one of us to work together to keep it a nice place to live.

There are many ways you and your family can help make positive changes for the ocean and the planet. For instance, you can start choosing sustainable seafood when you go to restaurants and the grocery store. Organizations such as Seafood Watch keep an updated online database of safe seafood choices. There is also a Seafood Watch smartphone app for making choices away from home.

A safe, sustainable seafood choice means the species is not in trouble due to overfishing. It also means the fish are being fished or farmed in ways that are not harming the surrounding ecosystem. If there's a fish dish on the menu that Seafood Watch labels Avoid, make another choice instead.

It matters what you and your family choose to order on a menu or buy at the store. The decision to buy sustainable seafood supports fisheries that make good choices for the environment, while also not supporting fisheries that aren't making good choices for the environment.

Another positive change you can start making today is to keep a closer eye on how you use resources such as electricity. Remember to turn lights, electronics, and appliances off when you're done using them. Did you know that many electrical devices that are plugged in use electricity even when they're off? Unplug these devices when no one is using them to eliminate this "vampire power."

Water is a precious resource that you can help conserve. To cut back on your water use, keep track of how long you're usually in the shower and then try to reduce that time by two or three minutes. If everyone in your family did this, you'd save a lot of water over the course of a year. Small changes can be easy to make, and, when taken all together, small changes add up to big results.

Humans must get from one place to another. Therefore, transportation is a massive way we are impacting the planet. Some families are helping by buying cars that use less fuel, by buying cars that run on electricity, or by carpooling. The best thing to do is to try to make the best possible choices for the environment every day. If it is safe for you to walk home from school, talk to a parent or guardian about the idea. If you can ride a bike to a friend's house instead of getting a ride in a car, ask a parent or guardian about the possibility.

The ocean would also be a lot better off if humans created less trash in the first place. "Reduce, reuse, and recycle" is a helpful saying to keep in mind. If we all started buying fewer things, reusing what we already have, and recycling what can be recycled, we'd be doing something great for the ocean.

When you're ready to make some changes, start by investing in a reusable water bottle so you don't have to use any more plastic water bottles. Next, see if you and your family can stop using plastic bags. Many grocery stores offer inexpensive reusable bags that you can take to the store and fill with groceries. That way, you don't need to bring new plastic or paper bags home each time you shop.

Create Ocean Creature Art

Ready to start reducing, reusing, and recycling? Start by reusing discarded items (trash) to create some ocean creature art. Envision and complete three crafts using safe trash and recyclable items made out of materials such as paper, plastic, cardboard, and Styrofoam. The key is to make your ocean creature crafts without creating any new trash.

YOU'LL NEED

◀ Various household trash and recyclables, such as:

> ✷ Egg cartons
>
> ✷ Cardboard tubes (such as empty paper towel and toilet paper rolls)
>
> ✷ Plastic bottles
>
> ✷ Soda cans
>
> ✷ Cereal boxes, Kleenex boxes, and other types of cardboard packaging
>
> ✷ Takeout food containers
>
> ✷ Paper and plastic bags

◀ Craft supplies (markers, paints, etc.)

◀ Adhesive (hot glue gun, glue stick, tape, etc.)

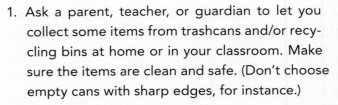

1. Ask a parent, teacher, or guardian to let you collect some items from trashcans and/or recycling bins at home or in your classroom. Make sure the items are clean and safe. (Don't choose empty cans with sharp edges, for instance.)

2. After a few days of collecting, lay your items out and start brainstorming about how you can reuse the items by turning them into something new.

3. Could you turn a paper towel roll into a hot-vent tubeworm? Could you use a Kleenex box as a sea turtle's shell? What could you use to make a sea jelly? Use the photos in this book as inspiration to build three ocean creatures from your trash.

4. Show off your creations to your friends or classmates and talk to them about reducing, reusing, and recycling.

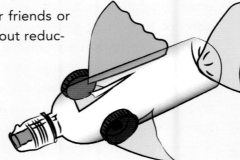

Consider using natural products that are free of chemicals that could end up in the water supply. If natural products are too expensive for your family budget, ask if your family can work together to make some natural products at home.

There are also more direct ways you and your family can help protect marine and freshwater ecosystems. You could do community service that helps the environment, such as cleaning up a local park or beach; you could volunteer your time at a zoo or aquarium to help spread conservation messages; you could participate in a citizen science project; or you could choose to buy products that have minimal packaging or that are made by businesses that are eco-friendly.

One of the most important ways you can start making a difference today is to do exactly what you're doing right now—learning! By learning about all the cool creatures and exciting places within our watery world, you're proving that you care about the ocean and the planet.

If you're wondering what to do after you finish reading this paragraph, it's easy: go share your new knowledge with others. When you're passionate about something, people will often listen. Write a book, sing a song, design an experiment, or do whatever it is you do best to share your love of marine science. When you do, you'll be making the world a better place.

You can make a difference for the ocean and all the animals that depend on it.
Courtesy of Beverly Houwing

Acknowledgments

Special thanks to our peer reviewer, Doug McCauley, and to *Mutual of Omaha's Wild Kingdom* host Stephanie Arne for the foreword. Thanks also to marine scientists Andrea Marshall, Asha de Vos, Emily Yam, Peter Edwards, and Randy Wells for donating time and effort.

This book would be much less exciting without the talents of Bryce Vrieling, our illustrator, and contributed photos from Beverly Houwing, Bruce Fryxell, Craig Smith, Joel Warburton, Lisa Hupp, Mark Gonka, Robin Riggs, and Ülar Tikk. Thanks to the Aquarium of the Pacific, MBARI, NOAA, and Polar Bears International for their support and to Jason Bruck and Whitlow Au for their expertise.

We're grateful for our enthusiastic activity testers: Michelle and Dylan; Erin, Noah, and Jake; Melissa, Andrew, and Ryan; Kenny; and the entire Frazier family. Finally, a big shout out to the team at Chicago Review Press for helping us bring our idea to life.

Courtesy of Mark Gonka

Glossary

adaptations In biology, traits that make an organism or species better able to live in its environment.

atmosphere The collection of gases that surrounds the planet.

atom The smallest and most basic unit of matter.

baleen Bristle-like tissue that is attached to the upper jaws of some whales and that filters plankton from seawater.

ballast water Water held in tanks aboard a ship that helps the ship stay stable during transit, sometimes transporting organisms from one ecosystem to another by accident.

biodiversity The diversity, or variety, of plant and animal life on Earth.

bioluminescence The production of light without creating heat by organisms.

breeding The process of producing offspring or young.

bycatch Unwanted species of fish or other marine life that are caught during fishing.

camouflage The result of an animal's form, coloring, patterning, or behavior that helps it avoid unwanted attention by blending in, appearing to be something it's not, or otherwise confusing predators.

chemosynthesis A process by which producers create energy they can use from chemical reactions as seen in hydrothermal vent communities.

citizen scientists People who engage in collecting data for scientific research, usually on a volunteer basis.

cold-blooded (ectothermic) Refers to animals, such as reptiles and most fish, whose body temperatures change along with the temperature of their environments.

commensalism A relationship between two organisms of different species in which one organism benefits and the other isn't affected.

conservation The attempt to preserve, restore, manage, or maintain a natural balance within an ecosystem.

consumer In ecology, an organism that eats other organisms, living or dead.

continental shelf The edge of a continent that's covered by a shallow area of sea.

coral bleaching The whitening of corals due to the loss of algae living in their tissues, often as a result of stress.

counterillumination A form of camouflage, similar to countershading, in which an organism produces light to match a faintly lit background.

countershading A form of coloration in which the upper areas of an organism's body are more darkly colored than the undersides.

current In marine science, the movement of water from one place to another because of wind, tides, water temperature, or salinity.

dam A barrier that holds water back and raises the water level on one side, creating a pond, lake, or reservoir.

data Facts, statistics, or other information for studying or referencing.

density The measure of the compactness of a substance, for instance, how much of something fits in a certain space.

echolocation An animal's ability to locate objects such as obstacles and prey using reflected sounds or echoes.

ecology The study of organisms' interactions with one another and with their environments.

ecosystem A natural unit made up of plants, animals, and their environments.

endangered (species) A threatened species with limited numbers left in the wild.

exoskeleton A hard covering that protects an organism's soft tissue.

extinct (species) A species that no longer exists on Earth.

fertilizer A substance that is added to the soil to help plants grow; it can be natural (like manure) or artificial (human-made).

food chain A sequence that traces how food energy gets transferred within an ecosystem as organisms eat and are eaten by other organisms.

fossils Preserved traces or remains of organisms from the past.

freshwater Water that does not contain a lot of salt, often stored in glaciers, rivers, lakes, and other inland bodies of water.

gills The organ some aquatic animals, such as fish, use to breathe underwater.

glacier A large, slowly moving mass of ice that stays frozen year-round, formed by years of snowfall.

global warming A slow temperature increase in Earth's atmosphere and oceans resulting from air pollution that traps heat.

habitat An area within an ecosystem where an organism lives.

harmful algae bloom An event marked by the overgrowth of phytoplankton in a body of water, which can be toxic or damaging to the ecosystem.

hydropower Electricity made from machines that are run by moving water.

hydrothermal vent An opening in the seafloor from which hot water flows, bringing minerals from Earth's core with it.

hypothesis A possible answer to a scientific question that can be tested by conducting an experiment or by gathering observations of the natural world.

invasive species An organism living in and sometimes causing damage to an environment where it is not native.

keystone species A species that plays a particularly important part in keeping its ecosystem healthy.

lateral line system A system of sensing organs in fish and amphibians that detects pressure changes, vibration, and movement in the surrounding water.

marine biology The scientific study of the plants and animals that live in or depend on the sea.

marine mammal An animal that is warm-blooded, has hair or fur, breathes air through lungs, bears live young, nurses its young, and has adapted to live all or part of its life in the water.

marine protected area (MPA) Aquatic area with rules in place to protect and preserve natural or cultural resources.

marine science The scientific study of the ocean, aquatic ecosystems, and aquatic life forms.

marine snow Small bits of waste and debris that slowly drift from the upper layers of the ocean to the seafloor.

metamorphosis The process by which an animal's form, function, and behavior change as it transforms into an adult, such as when a tadpole develops into a frog.

migration The seasonal movement of animals between two places.

mineral An inorganic (nonliving) substance formed naturally underground.

molecule The smallest amount of a substance that has all the features of that substance.

mutualism A relationship between two organisms of different species in which each organism benefits.

nymph An immature stage of an insect's life cycle.

ocean acidification A change in seawater's chemical makeup that makes it more acidic.

oceanic trench A steep-sided, narrow depression in the ocean floor.

parasitism A relationship between two organisms of different species in which one organism benefits by harming the other.

pesticides Toxic chemicals used to kill pests, such as insects.

photosynthesis A process by which producers capture energy from the sun and transform it into energy they can use.

plankton A collective term for marine and freshwater organisms that drift or weakly swim in a body of water.

plastic microbeads Tiny plastic beads used in products such as face scrubs and toothpastes that add to the plastic pollution in the ocean.

pollution The presence or introduction of a substance or object into the environment, including the land, water, and air, that makes it unsafe.

predator An organism that captures another organism for food.

prey An organism that is captured for food.

producer In ecology, an organism at the base of the food chain that gains energy from its physical environment—often the sun.

ROV (remotely operated vehicle) An unmanned underwater robot connected to a ship by a series of cables and operated by a crew on the ship.

salinity The amount of dissolved salts that are present in water.

scavenger A type of consumer that feeds on dead or dying matter.

scuba (self-contained underwater breathing apparatus) A device used for breathing while swimming underwater.

seamount A large submerged mountain, often an extinct volcano, that rises from the seafloor.

sonar A technique that uses sound waves and their echoes to detect objects and measure distances underwater.

spawn To reproduce by placing eggs or sperm into the water.

surface tension A property in which the molecules on the surface of a liquid hold onto each other to create an elastic-like layer.

tectonic plates Sections of the Earth's crust that move, often causing earthquakes and building volcanoes at their boundaries.

tide The changing level of the ocean caused by the gravity of the moon and the sun pulling on the Earth.

tissue In biology, a specialized collection of cells that make up the material of which animals are made.

upwelling The process by which warmer surface water is drawn away from shore and replaced by colder, nutrient-rich water from below.

venomous An animal that can produce venom and inject it, usually by bite or sting.

warm-blooded (endothermic) Refers to animals, such as mammals, that can maintain a stable body temperature even when the temperature of their environments change.

wavelength The distance between two corresponding points of a wave.

wetland An ecosystem on land, such as a marsh, swamp, or bog, in which the soil is saturated by water.

Resources

Association of Zoos and Aquariums (AZA)

www.aza.org

Use this site to find AZA-accredited zoos and aquariums.

Coral Restoration Foundation

www.coralrestoration.org

Learn about the science behind creating offshore nurseries and implementing restoration programs for threatened coral species.

International Union for Conservation of Nature (IUCN)

www.iucn.org

IUCN is a great resource for learning about environmental problems, worldwide conservation efforts, and endangered species.

Marine Megafauna Foundation

www.marinemegafauna.org

Find research, education, and conservation information about marine megafauna, including sharks, rays, sea turtles, and marine mammals that live along the coast of Mozambique.

Monterey Bay Aquarium Research Institute (MBARI)

www.mbari.org

Keep up to date with the latest scientific discoveries on MBARI's site, which is a hub for advanced research and education in ocean science and technology.

National Geographic Animals

www.nationalgeographic.com/animals

This site has a wealth of information on different animal species. Use it as a resource for many of the activities in this book.

NOAA Okeanos Explorer

www.oceanexplorer.noaa.gov/okeanos

Keep tabs on NOAA's expeditions and watch live as the *Okeanos Explorer* explores the seafloor.

Polar Bears International

www.polarbearsinternational.org

Polar Bears International is a go-to site for teachers and students who want to learn more about polar bears and the environmental issues that affect them.

Sarasota Dolphin Research Program

www.sarasotadolphin.org

Follow conservation scientists as they conduct long-term health studies on wild dolphins in Sarasota Bay.

Seafood Watch

www.seafoodwatch.org

Seafood Watch offers recommendations to help the public make sustainable seafood choices and support healthy ocean ecosystems.

Smithsonian Ocean Portal

www.ocean.si.edu

The Smithsonian Ocean Portal site is a helpful resource for learning more about ocean life and ecosystems, as well as conservation efforts.

United Nations Environment Programme (UNEP)

www.unep.org

Use this site to learn about international efforts to preserve and protect the natural world.

US Fish and Wildlife Service

www.fws.gov

Learn about coasts, wetlands, climate change, and endangered species. Find national wildlife refuges near you.

Woods Hole Oceanographic Institution (WHOI)

www.whoi.edu

Explore ocean topics—from hydrothermal vents and shipwrecks to coastal ecosystems and river systems.

World Wildlife Fund (WWF)

www.worldwildlife.org

Learn more about threatened ecosystems, including the ocean, freshwater systems, wetlands, and polar regions, as well as the animals that depend on these places.

Selected Bibliography

*Suitable for young readers.

Beebe, William. *Half Mile Down*. New York: Harcourt, Brace, 1934.

Broad, William J. *The Universe Below: Discovering the Secrets of the Deep Sea*. New York: Simon and Schuster, 1997.

*Burns, Loree Griffin. *Tracking Trash: Flotsam, Jetsam, and the Science of Ocean Motion*. New York: Houghton Mifflin, 2007.

Carson, Rachel. *The Sea Around Us*. New York: Oxford University Press, 1951.

Carson, Rachel. *Silent Spring*. New York: Houghton Mifflin, 1962.

Cawthorne, Nigel. *Shipwrecks: Disasters of the Deep Seas*. London: Arcturus, 2005.

Cramer, Deborah. *Smithsonian Ocean: Our Water, Our World*. New York: HarperCollins, 2008.

Diagram Group. *Marine Science: An Illustrated Guide to Science*. New York: Chelsea House, 2006.

*Doris, Ellen. *Marine Biology: Oceans, Shores, and Coastal Waters*. New York: Thames and Hudson, 1993.

Encyclopædia Britannica Online. www.britannica.com.

*Hall, David, and Mary Jo Rhodes. *Life on a Coral Reef*. New York: Scholastic, 2007.

*Hall, David, and Mary Jo Rhodes. *Life in a Kelp Forest*. New York: Scholastic, 2005.

*Hestermann, Josh, and Bethanie Hestermann. *Zoology for Kids: Understanding and Working with Animals*. Chicago: Chicago Review Press, 2015.

Hill, Amy Sauter. *Marine Biology: An Introduction to Ocean Ecosystems*. Portland, ME: Walch, 1995.

Hoffman, Jennifer. *Science 101: Ocean Science*. New York: HarperCollins, 2007.

Hutchinson, Stephen, and Lawrence E. Hawkins. *Oceans: A Visual Guide*. Richmond Hill, Ontario: Firefly Books, 2008.

*Knowlton, Nancy. *Citizens of the Sea: Wondrous Creatures from the Census of Marine Life*. Washington, DC: National Geographic Society, 2010.

Koslow, J. Anthony. *The Silent Deep: The Discovery, Ecology, and Conservation of the Deep Sea*. Chicago: University of Chicago Press, 2007.

*Littlefield, Cindy A. *Awesome Ocean Science*. Nashville: Williamson Books, 2003.

*Mason, Adrienne. *Oceans: Looking at Beaches and Coral Reefs, Tides and Currents, Sea Mammals and Fish, Seaweeds and Other Ocean Wonders*. Toronto: Kids Can Press, 1995.

Mladenov, Philip V. *Marine Biology: A Very Short Introduction*. New York: Oxford University Press, 2013.

*Price, Sean. *Water Pollution*. Tarrytown, NY: Marshall Cavendish Benchmark, 2009.

Shirihai, Hadoram, and Brett Jarrett. *Whales, Dolphins, and Other Marine Mammals of the World*. Princeton, NJ: Princeton University Press, 2006.

*Webb, Sophie. *Far from Shore: Chronicles of an Open Ocean Voyage*. New York: Houghton Mifflin Harcourt, 2011.

Webber, Herbert H., and Harold V. Thurman. *Marine Biology*. 2nd ed. New York: HarperCollins, 1991.

Index